MW01614310

This second book in the Spelling and Writing Together series helps children improve their spelling skills and learn to write more complex sentences. In the exercises, children construct sentences from words and phrases, combine short sentences into longer ones, and describe the action in single pictures and a series of pictures. Many exercises encourage children to express their own ideas, sometimes in response to pictures designed to stimulate their imagination. Spelling and writing lessons alternate. Every eighth lesson is a review.

A special note: Try not to correct children's misspellings of words that haven't been covered in the lessons. Children tend to be more imaginative and enthusiastic writers if they aren't limited to using only the words they know how to spell. If you wish, print the words so the children can see how they are spelled.

Table of Contents

Continued on next page

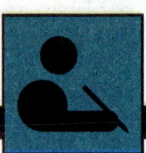

Glossary

Asking Sentence. A question.

Consonants. All the letters except **a, e, i, o, u,** and sometimes **y.**

Describing Words (Adjectives). Words that tell how something looks or feels, such as **happy**, **cold**, **hard**, and **tall**.

Doing Words (Verbs). Words that show action, such as **ride, carry, build,** and **grow.**

Joining Words (Conjunctions). Words that combine ideas in a sentence, such as **and, but, or, because**.

Sentence. A group of words that tells a whole idea or asks a question.

Vowels. The letters **a, e, i, o, u,** and sometimes **y.**

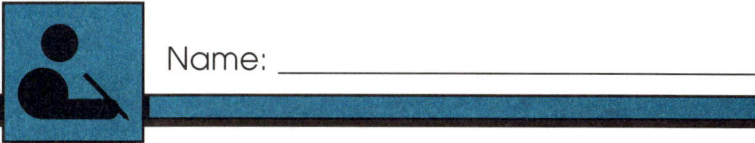

Name: _____

I Can Write Numbers!

Directions: Write each number beside the right picture. Then write it again.

one	two	three	four	five	six	seven	eight	nine	ten

Like this:

six six

I Know Which Ones Are Sentences!

A sentence tells a whole idea or asks a question.

Directions:

1. Read each group of words.
2. If it is a telling sentence, put a period at the end.
3. If it is an asking sentence, put a question mark.
4. If a word is missing, draw a line to the word that would finish the sentence. Put a period or question mark after the word.

Like this:

Did Peter's dog have ————————————— puppies?

1. Peter's dog had six

2. How old are the puppies now

                                                   mother

3. Do the puppies have names

                                                   puppies

4. The puppies still need to stay with their

5. There are three boy puppies and three

                                                   milk

6. Peter does not feed the puppies at all

7. What do puppies eat

                                                   walk

8. Their mother gives them

9. Peter has to take the mother dog for a

                                                girl puppies

10. Mom, may I have one of Peter's puppies

 Name: _____

I Know Which Words Rhyme!

Directions: Write the number word that rhymes.

Like this:

Billy really likes to run.
He is not the only _____.

<u>one</u>

| one | two | three | four | five | six | seven | eight | nine | ten |

1. My eyes are blue,
   And I have _____.

2. All my books fell on the floor,
   When I counted there were _____.

3. Should my picture have a tree?
   Yes, it should! I will draw _____.

4. My old cat can do some tricks.
   She can show you more than _____.

5. Don't be late!
   Be home by _____.

6. I was sick, but now I'm fine.
   May I please stay up 'til _____?

7. I'm lots older than my friend Ben.
   When he is nine, I will be _____.

I Can Change Sentences Around!

Directions: 1. Change the telling sentences into asking sentences. 2. Change the asking sentences into telling sentences. 3. Remember to start each one with a capital letter and end with a period or question mark.

Like this:

Is she eating three cookies?

She is eating three cookies.

He is bringing one truck.

Is he bringing one truck?

1. Is he painting two blue birds?

_____

_____

2. Did she find four apples?

_____

_____

3. She will be six on her birthday.

_____

_____

I Can Spell Number Words!

Directions: Write the right number words in the spaces.

one	two	three	four	five	six	seven	eight	nine	ten

1. Add a letter to each of these words to make a number word.
Like this:

even   on   tree

seven   _____   _____

2. Change a letter to make these words into number words.
Like this:

live   fix   line

five   _____   _____

3. Write the number words that sound the same as these:
Like this:

won   to   for

one   _____   _____

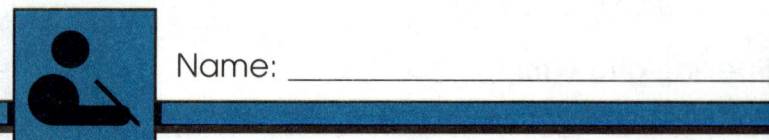

I Can Ask And Answer A Question!

Directions: Write a question about each picture. Begin with "how many." Then answer your question.

one	two	three	four	five	six	seven	eight	nine	ten

Like this:

How many cookies does the boy have? He has six cookies.

8

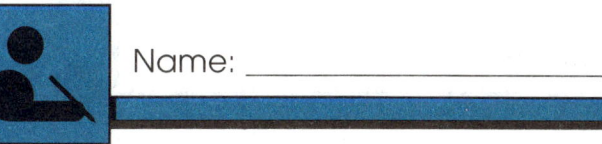

Name: _____

I Can Play A Word Game!

Directions: Look at the numbers in the squares in this word game. Then write the word that spells each number. Some words go down and some go across. Number one is done for you. Can you spell the other numbers by yourself?

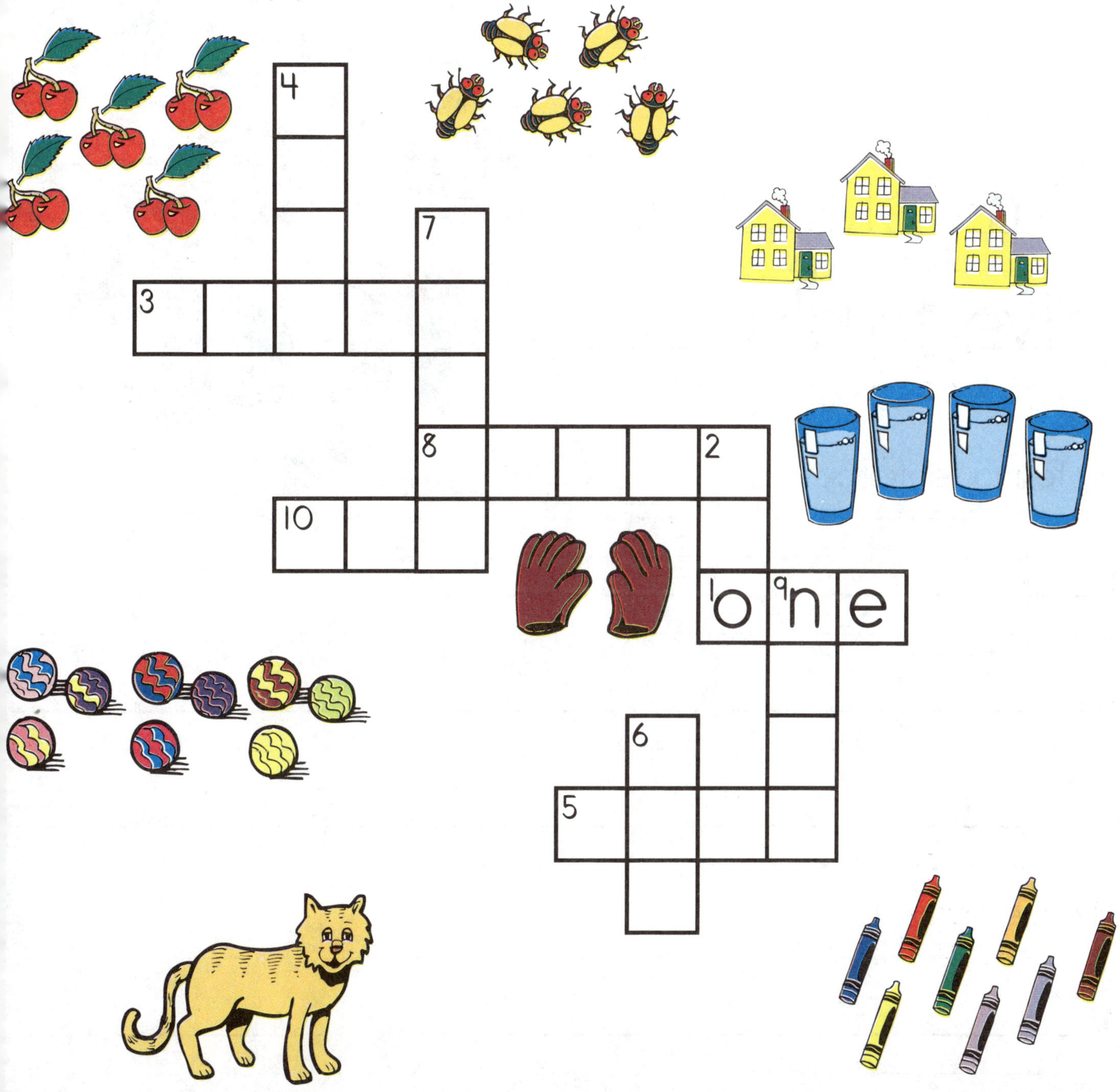

one

Copyright© 1995 American Education Publishing Co.

Name: _____

Review

Directions: Write three telling sentences and one asking sentence about this picture. Put a number word in each sentence. Then read your sentences to someone.

Like this:

This store has five trucks.

My telling sentences:

1. _____

_____

2. _____

_____

3. _____

_____

My question:

4. _____

_____

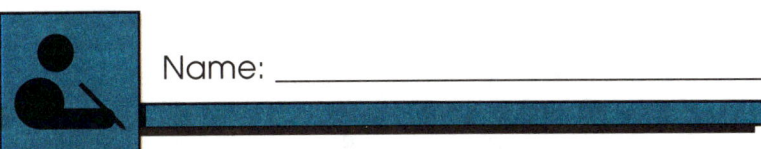

Name: _____

I Can Write the Names of Animals!

Directions: Write the name beside each picture. Then write it again.

| fox | rabbit | bear | woods | mouse | deer |

Like this:

squirrel   squirrel

Name: _____

I Know Where the Sentences Stop!

Directions: The words in each line are really two sentences. Draw a line between them. Write the two sentences again. Remember to start each one with a capital letter and put a period or question mark at the end.

Like this:

why do squirrels hide nuts / they eat them in the winter

Why do squirrels hide nuts?
They eat them in the winter.

1. bears sleep in the winter they don't need food then

_____

_____

_____

_____

2. he said he saw a fox do you think he did

_____

_____

_____

_____

Name: _____

I Know Special Ways to Spell Words!

To show two or more of something, we add **s** to most words.
Like this: one dog — **two dogs**   one book — **two books**

But some words are different. For words that end with **x**, use **es** to show two. Like this: one fox — **two foxes**   one box — **two boxes**

The spelling of some words changes a lot when there are two.
Like this: one mouse — **two mice**

Some words stay the same, even when you mean two of something.
Like this: one deer — **two deer**   one fish — **two fish**

Directions: Finish the sentences with the correct words. Some of them need just **s** to show two. Watch for the three words below.

deer — deer	mouse — mice	fox — foxes

1. The [rabbits] run fast. _____

2. The [deer] are eating. _____

3. Have you seen any [bears] today? _____

4. Where do the [foxes] live? _____

5. Did you ever have [mice] for pets? _____

Name: _____

I Can Write Two Kinds of Sentences!

Another name for an asking sentence is a **question**.

Directions: Use the words under the picture to write a telling sentence. Then add **do** to the words and write a question.

Like this:

a	mouse	I
see	the	bed
under		

Telling sentence:

I see a mouse under the bed.

Asking sentence (add **do**):

Do I see a mouse under the bed?

in	live
these	woods
bears	

Telling sentence:

_____
_____

Asking sentence (add **do**):

_____
_____
_____

I Can Find the Spelling Mistakes!

Directions: Circle the word in each sentence that is not spelled right. Then write the word correctly.

| woods | bear | rabbit | deer | fox | mouse |

Like this:
Animals like to live in the (threes).

trees

1. Bares do not eat people.

_____

2. They eat berries they find in the woulds.

_____

3. Sometimes a little moose might get into your house.

_____

4. Dear eat leaves and grass.

_____

5. A focks has a bushy tail.

_____

6. One day a rabitt came into our yard.

_____

Name: _____

I Can Make Two Sentences Into One!

Directions: Write the two short sentences as one sentence. Remember the special spelling of fox, mouse, and deer when there are two or more.

Like this:

I saw a mouse. You saw a mouse.

We saw two mice.

1. Julie petted a deer.
   Matt petted a deer.

_____

_____

_____

_____

2. Mike colored a fox.
   Kim colored a fox.

_____

_____

_____

_____

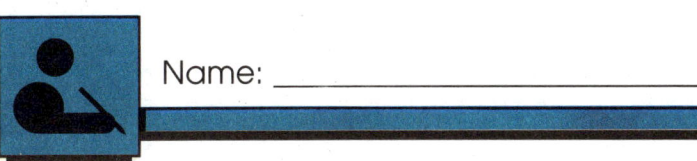

Name: _____

I Can Finish A Story!

Directions: Write the words that finish the story. Can you spell them by yourself now?

One day Kelly and I went for a walk in the _____

near my house. Kelly was a little afraid because her big brother told

her there was a _____ in the _____ .

"Don't worry," I told Kelly. "Only _____ and a

_____ or two live here." Just then we heard a noise in

the bushes. Kelly jumped, but it was just a _____

eating leaves. "I wasn't afraid," Kelly said when she saw it was just a

_____ "But I'm glad your dog came with us today."

"I don't have a dog!" I said. "Yes, you do!" Kelly said. "He's been

following us." She pointed behind me. It was a

_____ ! He was just watching us, but I was a little

afraid myself. "Kelly," I said quickly. "It's getting late. Let's go home!"

Review

Directions: Write two telling sentences and one question about the picture. Read your sentences to someone.

Like this:

How many rabbits
does she see?

My telling sentences:

1. _____

_____

_____

_____

2. _____

_____

_____

_____

My question:

_____

1. _____

_____

Name: _____

I Can Write "Family" Names!

Directions: This is Andy's **family tree**. It shows all the people in his family. Look at the pictures below that have names under them. Then find other pictures that are almost the same and write the same names under them.

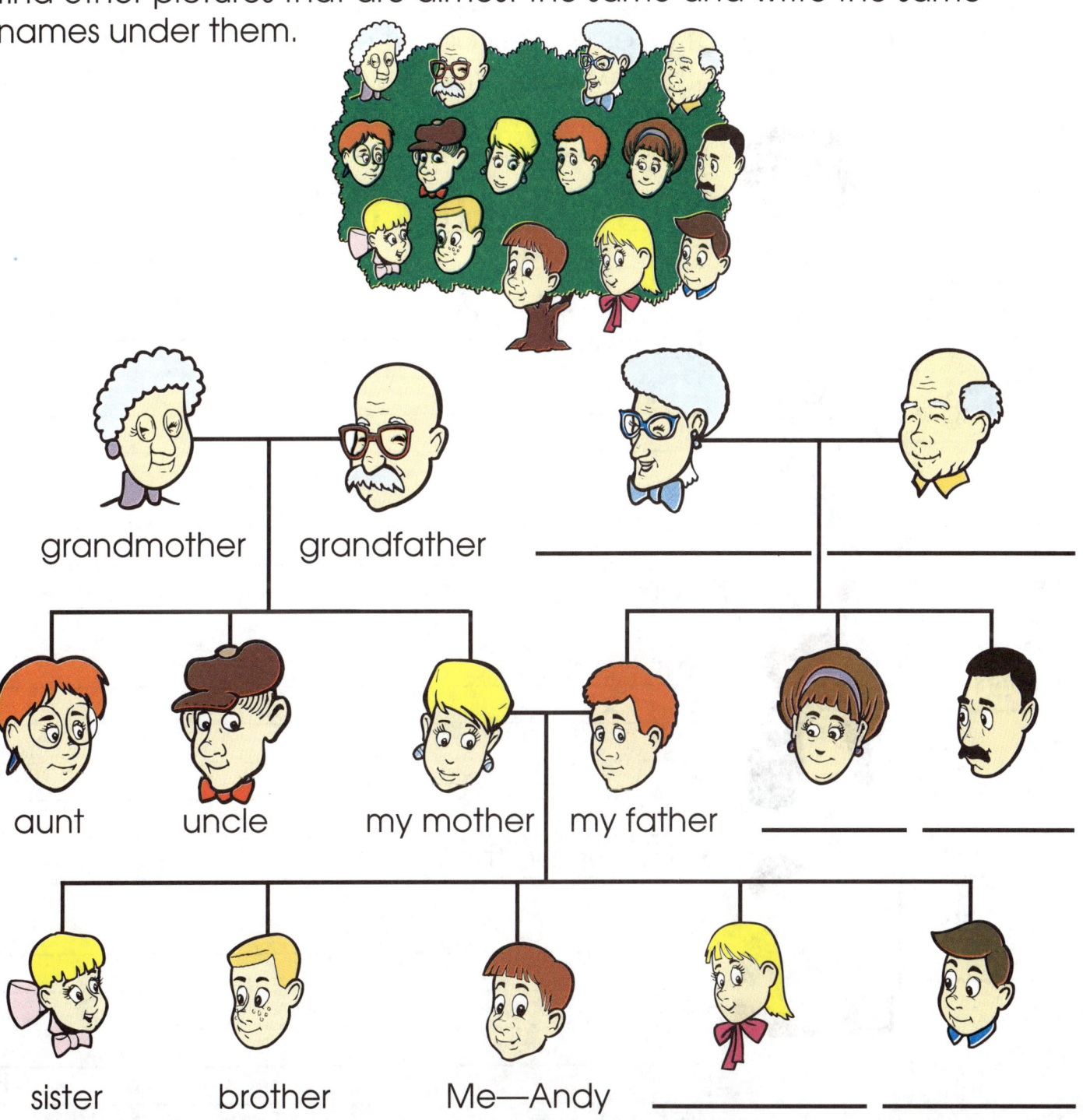

grandmother   grandfather   _____ _____

aunt   uncle   my mother   my father   _____ _____

sister   brother   Me—Andy   _____ _____

I Can Tell About People!

Some words tell how a person looks or feels. These are also called **describing** words.

Directions: Help Andy write about the people in his family. Cross out the **describing** word that does not tell about each picture. Write a sentence that uses the other two describing words.

Like this:

asleep
funny
tall

My aunt

is tall and funny.

fast
happy
smiling

1. My grandmother

_____
_____
_____
_____

hot
broken
tired

2. My uncle

_____
_____
_____

ready
hungry
hard

3. My little brother

_____
_____
_____
_____

Name: _____

I Know Which Letters Are Vowels!

Five letters are called vowels: **a**, **e**, **i**, **o**, and **u**. Sometimes **y** is also a vowel. All the rest of the letters are called consonants.

Directions: 1. In the first space, the vowels for each word are written for you. Add the consonants. 2. In the second space, the consonants are written. This time you add the vowels.

grandmother	grandfather	aunt	uncle	brother	sister

Like this:

mother

mo ther

o   e   br th r

a   a   e   gr ndf th r

u   e   ncl

i   e   s st r

a   o   e   gr ndm th r

au   nt

I Can Join Two Sentences!

You can join two short sentences to make one longer sentence. Three words help do this:

And —if both sentences are much the same.
Like this: I took my dog for a walk, **and** I played with my cat.

But —if the second sentence says something different from the first sentence. Sometimes the second sentence tells why you can't do the first sentence. **Like this:** I want to play outside, **but** it is raining.

Or —if each sentence names a different thing you could do.
Like this: You could eat your cookie, **or** you could give it to me.

Directions: Use the word given to join the two short sentences into one longer sentence.

Like this:
(but)
My aunt lives far away. She calls me often.

My aunt lives far away, but she calls me often.

1. (and)
My sister had a birthday. She got a new bike.

2. (or)
We can play outside. We can play inside.

Name: _____

I Can Spell "Family" Names!

Directions: Write the correct family names in the spaces.

grandmother	grandfather	aunt	uncle	brother	sister

1. Add one or more letters to these words to spell a family word.

Like this:

fat $\underline{father}$

ant   _____

is   _____

other   _____

and her _____

2. Write the family names that start the same as these words.

Like this:

$\underline{mother}$

_____

_____

_____

Name: _____

I Know Three "Joining" Words!

Directions: Read each set of sentences. Then join them with **and**, **but**, or **or**.

Like this:
My uncle likes popcorn.
He does not like peanuts.

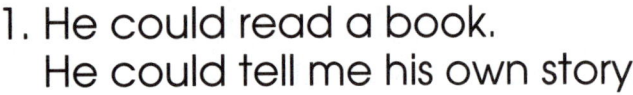

My uncle likes popcorn,
but he does not like peanuts.

1. He could read a book.
   He could tell me his own story.

_____

_____

_____

_____

2. My little brother is sleepy.
   He wants to go to bed.

_____

_____

_____

_____

Name: _____

I Can Finish A Story!

Directions: Write in the family words that finish the story. Can you spell them by yourself now?

One day my family had a picnic. My _____

baked chicken. _____ made some bread.

My _____ Jack brought corn. My _____

made something green and white in a big dish.

I ate chicken my _____ brought. I had two

rolls made by my _____ . My

_____ gave me some corn. I liked it all!

Then my _____ and I looked in the dish my

_____ had brought. "Did you try it?" I asked him.

"You're my big _____ ," he said. "You try it!" I put

a tiny bit in my mouth. It tasted good! But the dish was almost empty.

"It's terrible!" I said. "I'll eat the rest so you won't have to. That's what

a big _____ is for!" My _____

watched me eat it all. I tried not to look too happy!

Name: _____

Review

Directions: Draw a picture of everyone you can think of in your family. Write sentences that tell what you like about your brothers, sisters, aunts, uncles, grandmothers, and grandfathers. If you don't have any brothers or aunts or grandmothers, write a sentence telling that. (You can write more sentences on another piece of paper, if you run out of space.) Read your sentences to someone in your family.

My Family

My sentences:

_____

_____

_____

_____

_____

_____

_____

_____

_____

_____

_____

Name: _____

I Can Write More "Doing" Words!

Directions: Draw a line from each sentence to its picture. Then finish the sentence with the **doing** word that is under the picture.

Like this:

He will ____help____ the baby.

carry

help

1. I can _____ my book.

cut

2. It is time to _____ up.

build

3. That chair will _____ .

clean

4. They _____ houses.

fix

5. I _____ this out myself.

break

6. Is that too heavy to _____ ?

I Can Write Long Sentences!

Directions: 1. Join each pair of sentences to make one longer sentence. Use one of the **joining** words: **and**, **but**, **or**. 2. In the second part of the sentence, use **he**, **she**, or **they** in place of a person's name.

Like this: I asked Tim to help me. Tim wanted to play.

I asked Tim to help me, but
he wanted to play.

1. Kelly dropped a glass.
   Kelly cut her finger.

_____

_____

_____

2. Linda got a new dog.
   Linda named it Baby.

_____

_____

_____

_____

Name: _____

I Can Spell These "Doing" Words!

Directions: Write the correct **doing** words in the spaces.

break	build	fix	clean	cut	carry

1. Change one letter in each word to make it a **doing** word.

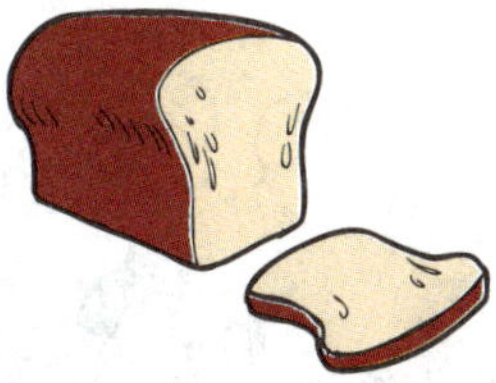

_____
_____
_____
_____
_____
_____
_____
_____
_____

2. Which **doing** word:

Starts like cow and
ends the same as every?

_____
_____

Starts and ends the
same as fox?

_____
_____

Starts like boy and
ends the same as red?

_____
_____

Starts and ends the
same as corn?

_____
_____

Starts like birthday and
ends the same as quick?

_____
_____
_____

Name: _____

I Can Write What Happens!

Directions: In each story, one picture does not have a sentence. Write a sentence that tells what happened in that picture. Use one of the **doing** words.

break	build	fix	clean	cut	carry

 Today is Mike's birthday.

Mike asked four friends to come.

 _____
_____
_____

 Amy's dog walked in the mud.

He got mud in the house.

  _____
_____
_____

Name: _____

I Can Change The Spelling!

Most **doing** words end with **s** when the sentence tells about one thing. The **s** is taken away when the sentence tells about more than one thing.

Like this:

One dog walks.   Two dogs walk.
One boy runs.   Three boys run.

The spelling of some **doing** words changes when the sentence tells about only one thing.

Like this:

One girl carries her lunch.   Two girls carry their lunches.
The boy fixes his car.   Two boys fix their cars.

(The spelling for **fix** and **fixes** is just like **fox** and **foxes**.)

Directions: Write the missing **doing** words in the sentences.

Like this:

Pam works hard. She and Peter __work__ all day.

1. The father bird builds a nest. The mother and father _____ it together.

2. The girls clean their room. Jenny _____ under the bed.

3. The children cut out their pictures. Henry _____ his slowly.

4. These workers fix things. This man _____ televisions.

5. Two trucks carry horses. One truck _____ pigs.

31

I Can Tell A Story!

Directions: Write a sentence that tells what happens in each picture. Use the **doing** word printed under the picture. Remember the spelling changes in the lesson on page 211. Read your story  to someone.

Like this:

fall    **break**    **clean**

A glass falls off the table.

_____

_____

_____

_____

_____

fix    **cut**    **carry**

_____

_____

_____

_____

_____

_____

Name: _____

I Can Find the Spelling Mistakes!

Directions: Circle the two spelling mistakes in each sentence. Then write the sentence correctly. Watch for mistakes in **doing** words, family names, animals, and numbers. Can you spell the words by yourself now?

Like this:

I need to (klean) the cage my (mouses) live in.

I need to clean the cage my mice live in.

2. The chair will brake if tree of us sit on it.

3. A mother bare carry her baby in her mouth.

Review

Directions: Write sentences that answer the questions under each picture. Be sure to use the **doing** words.

What will happen here? What will the boy do next?

_____

_____

_____

_____

_____

_____

_____

How is the girl helping? What will happen next?

_____

_____

_____

_____

_____

_____

_____

_____

_____

Name: _____

I Can Write Words That Tell "Where"!

Directions: Draw a line from each sentence to its picture. Then finish each sentence with the word under the picture.

Like this:

He is walking _____behind_____ the tree.

outside

1. We stay _____ when it rains.

behind

between

2. She drew a dog _____ his house.

across

3. She stands _____ her friends.

around

4. They walked _____ the bridge.

beside

5. Let the cat go _____ .

inside

6. Draw a circle _____ the fish.

Name: _____

I Know Which Word To Write!

Directions: Use one of the **where** words to finish each sentence. The pictures will help you know which word to use.

between	around	inside	outside	beside	across

Like this:

She will hide ____under____ the basket.

1. In the summer we like to play _____ in the park.

2. She can swim _____ the lake.

3. Put the bird _____ its cage so it won't fly away.

4. Sit _____ Bill and me so we can all work together.

5. Your picture is right _____ mine on the wall.

6. The fence goes _____ the house.

Name: _____

I Know The "Where" Words!

Directions: Write the **where** words that answer the questions.

| between | around | inside | outside | beside | across |

1. Write all the little words you find in the **where** words.

_____

_____

_____

_____

_____

2. Which two words start with  ?

_____   _____

_____   _____

3. Which words are these?

a +    _____

_____

_____

a + ✝   _____

_____

4. Write three words that rhyme with  **hide**

_____ _____ _____

_____ _____ _____

_____ _____ _____

I Can Write My Own Sentences!

between	around	inside	outside	beside	across

the yard	the house	the table	the school	the box
the hill	the picture	the field	the puddle	the park

Directions: Finish each sentence with a **where** word from the top word box and add more words from the bottom word box. You can use other words, too.

Like this:

Our garden grows <u>outside in the yard</u> .

1. We like to play _____ .

2. The street goes _____ .

3. Can you run _____ ?

4. Let's ride bikes _____ .

Pick one sentence and draw a picture about it:

Name: _____

I Remember the Vowels!

The vowels are **a**, **e**, **i**, **o**, **u**, and sometimes **y**. All the other letters are consonants.

Directions: In the first space are the vowels for each **where** word. In the second space are the consonants for the same word. Fill in the missing letters.

between	around	inside	outside	beside	across

Like this:

behind    behind

a _ ou   r _ nd

e i _ e   b _ s _ d

i _ i _ e   ns _ d

ou _ i _ e   ts _ d

e _ ee   b _ tw _ n

a _ o   cr _ ss

Name: _____

I Can Write Long Sentences!

Directions: Join each pair of sentences to make a longer sentence. Use one of the **joining** words: **and**, **but**, **or**.

Like this: We play outside when it is sunny.
Today it is raining.

We play outside when it is sunny, but today it is raining.

1. We could walk between the buildings. We could walk around them.

_____

_____

_____

_____

_____

2. I drew a tree beside the house. I drew flowers beside the house.

_____

_____

_____

_____

_____

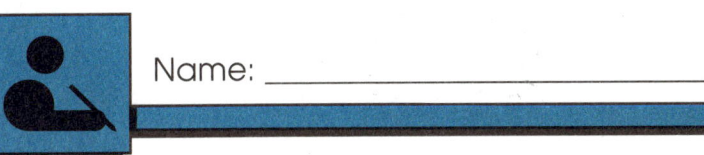

Name: _____

I Can Spell Words That Tell "Where"!

Directions: Write the words that tell where the cat is. Use each **where** word once. Can you spell them by yourself now?

Like this:

Where is this cat?

Where is this cat?

Where is this cat?

Where is this cat?

Where is this cat?

The cat is behind the box.

Name: _____

Review

Directions: Write sentences about this picture. Use the **where** words you know. Then read your sentences to someone.

Here are some more words you can use: **monkey**, **rope**, **fence**, **zoo**, **cage**.

_____

_____

_____

_____

_____

_____

_____

_____

_____

_____

_____

_____

_____

_____

_____

_____

_____

_____

Name: _____

I Can Write More "Opposite" Words!

Directions: Draw a line from each sentence to its picture. Then finish each sentence with the word under the picture.

Like this:

hard

She bought a _____ new _____ bat.

new

1. I like my _____ pillow.

top

2. Birthdays make me _____ .

sad

3. Put that book on _____ .

slowly

4. Jenny runs _____ .

quickly

5. A rock makes a _____ seat.

happy

6. I feel _____ when it rains.

soft

7. He eats _____ .

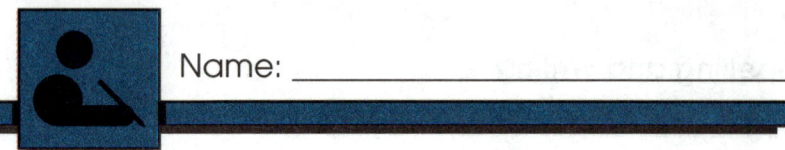

Name: _____

I Can Use "Opposite" Words In Sentences!

Directions: Use each **opposite** word once to finish these sentences.

| hard happy top cold soft quickly hot bottom sad slowly |

Like this:

My new coat is blue on _____top_____ and

red on the __bottom__ .

1. Snow is _____ , but fire is _____ .

2. A rabbit runs _____ , but a turtle

moves _____ .

3. A bed is _____ , but the floor is _____ .

4. I feel _____ when my friends come

and _____ when they leave.

Name: _____

I Know The Sounds In "Opposite" Words!

Directions: Write the **opposite** words that answer the questions.

hard	happy	top	soft	quickly	bottom	sad	slowly

1. Which word rhymes with glad and is the opposite of it?

_____
_____

2. Which words start the same as [SOAP] ?

_____
_____
_____
_____

_____

3. Take one letter out of each word to make it an **opposite** word.

_____

stop

_____
_____

heard

_____
_____

said

_____

4. Add consonants to these vowels to make three **opposite** words.

u i _ _ y   _ o _ o   _ a _ y

Name: _____

I Can Write My Own Sentences!

Directions: Read the words in the box beside each picture. Cross out the word that does not tell about the picture. Write a sentence about the picture using the other two words.

Like this:

~~Doll~~	garden	digs

She digs in her garden.

swims	quickly	five

_____
_____
_____
_____
_____
_____

soft	fly	happy

_____
_____
_____
_____
_____
_____

popcorn	bottom	sad

_____
_____
_____
_____
_____
_____

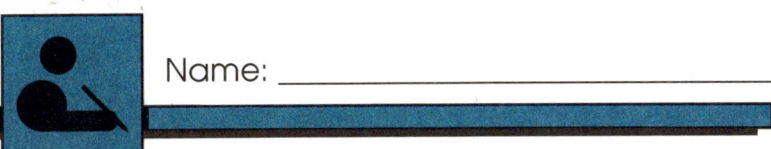

Name: _____

I Can Finish A Story!

Directions: Write in the words that finish the story. Remember that some of the words start the same.

| hard | happy | top | soft | quickly | bottom | sad | slowly |

One day Grandma came for a visit. She gave my sister Jenny and

me a box of chocolate candy. We said, "Thank you!" Then Jenny

__q_____ took the __t_____ off the box. The pieces all

looked the same! I couldn't tell which pieces were __h_____

inside and which were __s_____ ! I only liked the

__s_____ ones. Jenny didn't care. She was __h_____

to get any kind of candy!

I __s_____ looked at all the pieces. I didn't know which one

to pick. Just then Dad called us. Grandma was going home. He

wanted us to say good-bye to her. I hurried to the front door where

they were standing. Jenny came a minute later.

I told Grandma I hoped I would see her soon. I always felt

__s_____ when she left. Jenny stood behind me and didn't

say anything. After Grandma went home, I found out why. Jenny had

most of our candy in her mouth! Only a few pieces were left in the

__b_____ of the box! Then I was __s_____ ! That Jenny!

I Can Tell About Something!

Directions: Look at each picture. Then write a sentence that uses the word under the picture. Tell how something is the same as the picture.

Like this:

cold

My hands are as cold as ice.

hard

slowly

quickly

happy

Name: _____

I Can Do A Word Game!

Directions: Read the sentence by each number and think of a word that would finish it. Write the word in the spaces starting with the same number. The first letter is filled in for you. Can you spell the rest of the word by yourself now?

Words that go down:

1. Put the biggest box on the ____.
3. The rabbit runs ____.
4. When my friend moved away, I felt ____.
5. Sunny days make me ____.

Words that go across:

2. Put the smallest box on the ____.
4. Kittens feel warm and ____.
6. Turtles feel ____.
7. Grandpa walks ____.

Spelling and Writing

Name: _____

Review

Directions: Tell a story about the picture by following the directions. Write one or two sentences for each answer.

1. Tell about something happy in the picture.
_____
_____
_____

2. Now tell about something sad.
_____
_____

3. Write about something that is happening quickly or slowly.
_____
_____

4. Use **top** or **bottom** in a sentence about the picture.
_____
_____

5. Tell about something hard and something soft in the picture.Use **but** in your sentence.
_____
_____
_____
_____

Name: _____

I Can Write Words About Learning!

Directions: Write the correct word to finish each sentence. Use each word only once. The first letter is done for you.

start	watch	listen	teach	finish	write

1. You see with your eyes, but you l_____ with your ears.

2. After you think of an idea, W_____ it on your paper.

3. I will t_____ you how to write your name.

4. To see what to do, you have to W_____ the teacher.

5. Show me your picture after you f_____ drawing it.

6. When you have everything you need, you can S_____ working.

Name: _____

I Know Which Part Tells Why!

Some sentences explain things. They use the word **because**.

Directions: Draw a line from the first part of each sentence to the ending that explains why.

1. Let's watch Tim because   I miss her.

2. Kelly will teach us how to   it started to rain.
   skate because

3. I can't start painting because   I don't have any paints.

4. We could not finish the   she is a good skater.
   baseball game because

5. I will write to Grandmother   he knows how to play
   because   this game.

6. I could not listen because   everyone was making
                                               too much noise.

Name: _____

Spelling I Can Spell Words About Learning!

Directions: Write the words that answer the questions.

start	watch	listen	teach	finish	write

Which words are not spelled correctly? Circle them and then write them correctly.

1. Do you like to wach television? _____

_____

2. Right your name at the bottom. _____

_____

3. I will teech you to ride a bike. _____

_____

4. You have to lisen to me. _____

_____

5. Did you finnish reading your book? _____

_____

6. Everyone will strat running at the same time. _____

Change one letter in each word below to make one of the **learning** words. Write the new word on the line.

reach   white   match

_____   _____   _____

_____   _____   _____

_____   _____   _____

Name: _____

I Can Tell Why!

Directions: Write your own ending to the sentences below. Tell why something happened.

Like this:

I will read this book because

I like stories about baseball.

1. We have to finish quickly because

_____

_____

_____

2. I want to watch television because

_____

_____

_____

3. Please write a letter to me because

_____

_____

_____

 4. I'm going to start eating more because

_____

_____

_____

Name: _____

I Know Different Ways To End Words!

Remember that **doing** words end with **s** when the sentence tells about only one thing.

Like this: One girl reads.   Two girls read.

But when a **doing** word ends with **ch** or **sh**, add **es**.

Like this: She watches the baby.   We watch the baby, too.
       Peter finishes his work.   Jane and Sue finish their work.

Directions: Write the word that finishes each sentence.

Like this:
   Carrie reads the book. She and Chris ____read____ it together.

| start | watch | listen | teach | finish | write |

1. Todd listens to the teacher. We all _____ to her.

2. Joy finishes the race first. We _____ after her.

3. They write letters to our class. Tony _____ back to them.

4. We watch the puppet show. She _____ with us.

5. He starts at the top of the page. We _____ in the middle.

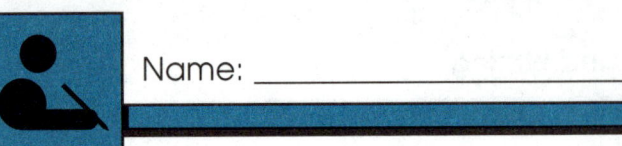

Name: _____

I Can Write My Own Sentences!

Directions: Write your own sentences. Use a word from each box and add more words of your own to finish your sentences. Add **s** or **es** to the end of the **doing** words if you need to. Use **because** in one of your sentences. Draw a picture to show what is happening in one sentence.

teach	write	listen	watch	start	finish

We	She	They	He	Kenny	Susan
Tammy	Henry	(other names you know)			

Like this:

1. Robert watches the race.

2. _____

3. _____

4. _____

Draw your picture here:

I Can Finish A Story!

Directions: Write in the **learning** words that finish this story. The first letter of each one is written for you. Can you spell the rest by yourself?

    "How can I t_____ you anything if you don't

l_____ ?" James asked his little sister Wendy. He was trying

to show her how to w_____ her name. Wendy smiled up at

James. "I'll l_____ now," she said. "Okay. Let's

s_____ again. W_____ what I do," he said.

"First, you make a big **W**." "Up and down," Wendy said.

She tried to w_____ a **W** like James, but it

looked like a row of upside-down mountains.

"That's better," James said. "But you have to know when to stop." He

showed her how to w_____ **e**, **n**, and **d**. "Now I'll

t_____ you how to f_____ your name," he said.

He wrote a **y** for her. Wendy made the tail on her **y** go down to the

bottom of the page. "I can do it!" she said. "I can w_____

my name from s_____ to f_____ !" She smiled at

her brother again. "Would you t_____ me how to read

now, James?" He smiled back at her. "Maybe later, okay?"

Review

Directions: Answer the questions below to tell your own story about this picture. Use the **learning** words you know.

1. What are these children going to do?

_____

_____

_____

_____

2. What are the boy and girl at the front of the class talking about?

_____

_____

3. What will happen next?

_____

_____

4. What will the children sitting on the boxes do?

_____

_____

5. What would you tell the children sitting on the boxes if you were the teacher here?

_____

_____

_____

_____

_____

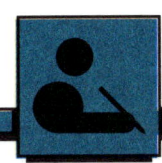

Name: _____

I Can Write "Time" Words!

The time between breakfast and lunch is **morning**.

The time between lunch and dinner is **afternoon**.

The time between dinner and bedtime is **evening**.

Directions: Write the correct word to finish each sentence. Use each word only once.

evening	morning	today	tomorrow	afternoon

1. What did you eat for breakfast

   this _____ ?

2. We come home from school in the _____ .

3. I help wash the dinner dishes in

   the _____ .

4. I feel a little tired _____ .

5. If I rest tonight, I will feel better _____ .

Name: _____

I Can Write Long Sentences!

Directions: Make each pair of short sentences into one long sentence. Use these joining words: **and, but, or, because**.

Like this:

This morning I am sleepy. I stayed up late last night.

This morning I am sleepy because I stayed up late last night.

1. Do you want to go in the morning?
   Do you want to go in the afternoon?

_____

_____

_____

_____

2. Mom asked me to clean my room today. I forgot.

_____

_____

_____

_____

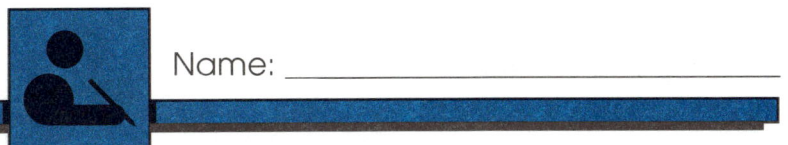

Name: _____

I Know Vowels and Consonants!

Directions: The vowels for each **time** word are written on the first space. The consonants for the same word are on the second space. Write in the missing letters for all the words.

Like this:

morning	afternoon	evening	today	tomorrow

night   night

o   i   m   rn   ng

a   e   oo   ft   rn   n

e   e i g   v   n   ng

o   a   t   d   y

o   o   o   t   m   rr   w

Name: _____

I Can Write My Own Sentences!

Directions: Write a sentence for these **time** words.
Tell something you do at that time.

Like this:

day

Every day I walk to school.

morning

_____

afternoon

_____

evening

_____

62

I Can Do A Word Game!

Directions: The words by each number tell about one of the **time** words. Write the right **time** word by the same number in the game. Can you spell the words by yourself now?

The word that goes down:
1. The time between lunch and dinner

The words that go across:
2. This day
3. The next day
4. The time between breakfast and lunch
5. The time between lunch and bedtime

Name: _____

Review

Directions: Write the story below again and fix all the mistakes. Watch for: words that aren't spelled right; missing periods and question marks; question marks at the end of telling sentences; sentences with the wrong **joining** words. If needed, use your own paper, too.

One mourning my granmother said I could have a pet mouse. She would teech me how to take care of it. First, she helped me bild a cage. I said I would keep it very klean?

That evenening we got my mouse at the pet store, the next afernoon my mouse had babies! Now I had nyne mouses! I really liked to wach them? I wanted to pick the babies up, and they were too little.

When they get bigger, I have to give too mouses to my sisster. Maybe her mouses will have babies, but we will have more mouses!

_____

_____

_____

_____

_____

_____

_____

_____

_____

_____

_____

_____

_____

_____

_____

_____

What Happened Here?

Look at this picture.
Work with a grown-up to answer the questions.
Try to find out what happened.

What time of day is it? _____

How do you know? _____

Why is the picnic basket open? _____

Why is the family upset? _____

Where is the picnic food? _____

What will the family do now? _____

Write a short story to go with the picture.
Tell the story to your grown-up.
Your grown-up will help you write your story.
Write your story on another sheet of paper.

What Will Happen?

Do this with a grown-up.
Read this story out loud to your grown-up.

Pam and Sam are twins. They are at home
alone after school. They know they should not
play ball in the living room, but they play
anyway. They are having a great time. Then Pam
throws the ball to Sam, but Sam misses it. The
ball crashes into Mom's best red and white vase.
The vase falls down. The vase smashes to bits.
Water, a rose, and pieces of red and white vase
cover the floor. What a mess!

What will happen next?
Write your idea here.
Tell your grown-up to write his or her idea on another paper.

_____

_____

_____

_____

_____

_____

_____

My Friend

Do this with a grown-up.
Some people make good friends.
Some people do not make good friends.
Here are some famous people.
Read each name.
Decide if you would like the person for a friend.
Write the reason you have this feeling.
Then let your grown-up decide.

Cinderella

Would you like Cinderella for a friend? _____

Why? _____

Would your grown-up like Cinderella for a friend? _____

Why? _____

Humpty-Dumpty

Would you like Humpty-Dumpty for a friend? _____

Why? _____

Would your grown-up like Humpty-Dumpty for a friend? _____

Why? _____

Hansel and Gretel

Would you like Hansel and Gretel for friends? _____

Why? _____

Would your grown-up like Hansel and Gretel for friends? _____

Why? _____

Analyzing characters

Is It True?

Do this with a grown-up.
Read the three animal stories below.
Two of the stories are true. One story is not true.
Decide if a story is true or not true.
You and your grown-up will circle your answer choices.

Crabs protect themselves in a strange way. If an enemy grabs a crab by the leg, the crab lets its leg fall off. Later it grows a new leg.

I think this story is   true   not true
My grown-up thinks this story is   true   not true

Camels live in the desert and sometimes go without food for many days. The camel has a hump filled with fat. The camel lives off the fat in its hump until it can get more food.

I think this story is   true   not true
My grown-up thinks this story is   true   not true

The wood turtle crawls out of its shell to hunt for bugs that live in the trees. Then it goes back in its shell to eat the bugs.

I think this story is   true   not true
My grown-up thinks this story is   true   not true

Each sentence below tells about one of the animal stories.
If the sentence gives the main idea of the story, the story is true.
If the sentence does not give the main idea, the story is not true.

1. A crab will drop off a leg to protect itself.
2. Fat in a camel's hump helps keep it alive.
3. Turtles eat bugs.

Follow the Plan

Here are two story plans. Read them both.
Which plan do you like better?
On a sheet of paper, write a story to fit your favorite plan.

PLAN 1

What the story is about: Kate grows a flower. Her
flower can talk. Her flower can do magic.

The problem: Kate wants to keep her magic flower
a secret, but the flower talks and talks.

Important characters: Kate
the flower
Kate's teacher

An important fact: The flower grows legs and
follows Kate to school.

PLAN 2

What the story is about: Fluzz is an elf who likes to
tease. He lives in the kingdom of Muzz. Fluzz
has been sleeping for 100 years. When he is
asleep, all is well. When Fluzz wakes up, he
begins to tease. Then everyone is unhappy.

The problem: Fluzz wakes up today.

Important characters: Fluzz
the queen
the princess

Two important facts: The princess is 7 years old.
Fluzz loves to sing songs.

Using a story plan

69

Interview

Find out some true things about your grown-up.
Read each question to your grown-up.
Tell your grown-up to give you
a true answer to each question.
Write down every answer.
They should all be true,
or **nonfiction**.

Where did you grow up?

_____

Did you live in a house or an apartment?

_____

Did you have any pets when you were growing up?

_____

What did you like about school?

_____

What didn't you like about school?

_____

What did you like to do out of school?

_____

What was your favorite food when you were growing up?

_____

When you were little, what did you want to be when you grew up?

_____

Goo or Roo?

Giants from the land of Goo say things that are true.
Giants from Roo say things that could never be true.
Read what each giant says.
Is the giant from Goo or Roo?
Circle your answer.

Last week I had a melted cheese sandwich.

I am from:

Goo   Roo

Yesterday your teacher flew to school on a bird.

I am from:

Goo   Roo

Tomorrow all the rivers on earth will turn to gold.

I am from:

Goo   Roo

Many children like to play with blocks.

I am from:

Goo   Roo

You can get books about monsters at the library.

I am from:

Goo   Roo

If you eat too many peas, you will turn green.

I am from:

Goo   Roo

Write something a giant from Goo might say.

_____

Write something a giant from Roo might say.

_____

Distinguishing between reality and fantasy

Could It Be?

Do this with a grown-up.
Take turns.
Toss a coin.
If you get heads, cross out a sentence that could be true.
If you get tails, cross out a sentence that could not be true.
The first player who cannot find a sentence to cross out
loses the game.
If all the sentences are crossed out, it is a tie game.

Pearl wants to be a doctor when she grows up.

Joan likes to swim.

It rained all last night.

Tim turns invisible when he eats oatmeal.

A robot turned Leon's frog into a horse.

Jim rode his bike to school.

It rained gold rings last night.

Keisha rang a bell and her chair started flying around the room.

Pablo likes to eat popcorn.

Earl's cat can talk Spanish.

Carmen went to live on the moon for a year.

Roberto did his homework after dinner.

ANSWER KEY

MASTER SPELLING/WRITING
2

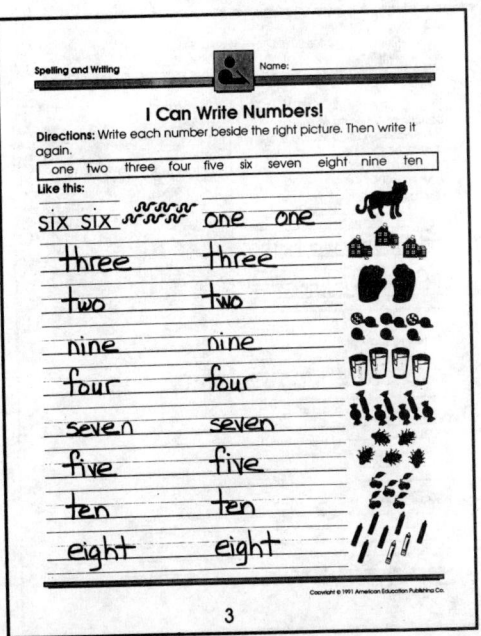

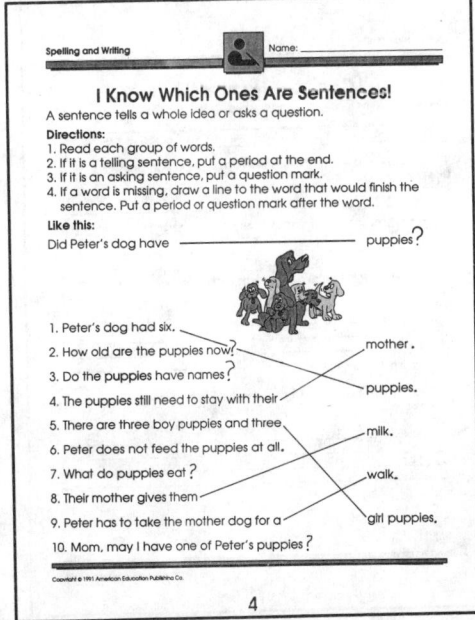

I Know Which Words Rhyme!

Directions: Write the number word that rhymes.

Like this:

Billy really likes to run.
He is not the only _____. **one**

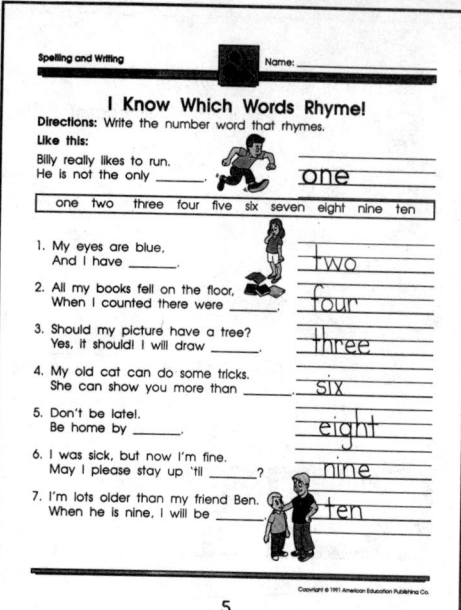

| one | two | three | four | five | six | seven | eight | nine | ten |

1. My eyes are blue,
   And I have _____. **two**

2. All my books fell on the floor,
   When I counted there were _____. **four**

3. Should my picture have a tree?
   Yes, it should! I will draw _____. **three**

4. My old cat can do some tricks.
   She can show you more than _____. **six**

5. Don't be late!
   Be home by _____. **eight**

6. I was sick, but now I'm fine.
   May I please stay up 'til _____? **nine**

7. I'm lots older than my friend Ben.
   When he is nine, I will be _____. **ten**

5

I Can Change Sentences Around!

Directions: 1. Change the telling sentences into asking sentences. 2. Change the asking sentences into telling sentences. 3. Remember to start each one with a capital letter and end with a period or question mark.

Like this:

is she eating three cookies?

She is eating three cookies.

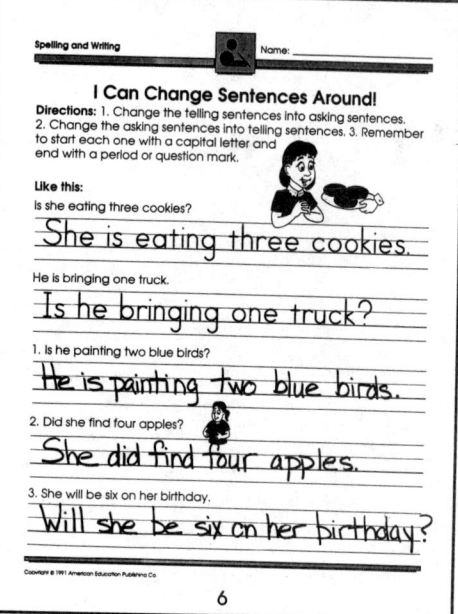

He is bringing one truck.

Is he bringing one truck?

1. Is he painting two blue birds?

He is painting two blue birds.

2. Did she find four apples?

She did find four apples.

3. She will be six on her birthday.

Will she be six on her birthday?

6

I Can Spell Number Words!

Directions: Write the right number words in the spaces.

| one | two | three | four | five | six | seven | eight | nine | ten |

1. Add a letter to each of these words to make a number word.
Like this:

even **seven**   on **one**   tree **three**

2. Change a letter to make these words into number words.
Like this:

live **five**   fix **six**   line **nine**

3. Write the number words that sound the same as these:
Like this:

won **one**   to **two**   for **four**

7

I Can Ask And Answer A Question!

Directions: Write a question about each picture. Begin with "how many." Then answer your question.

| one | two | three | four | five | six | seven | eight | nine | ten |

Like this:

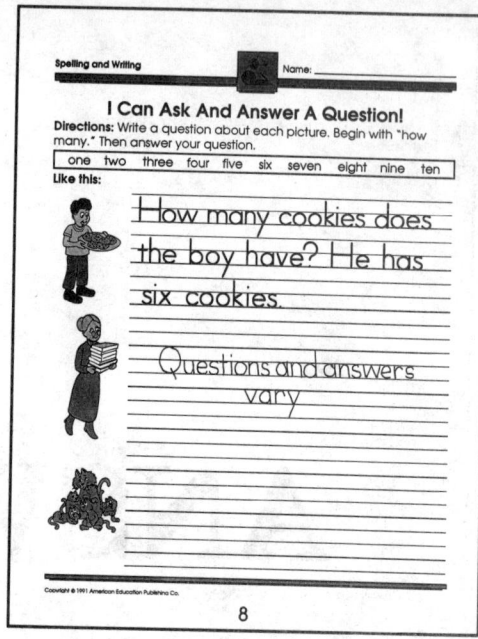

How many cookies does the boy have? He has six cookies.

Questions and answers vary

8

I Can Play A Word Game!

Directions: Look at the numbers by the squares in this word game. Then write the word that spells each number. Some words go down and some go across. Number one is done for you. Can you spell the other numbers by yourself?

9

Look What I Can Write!

Directions: Write three telling sentences and one asking sentence about this picture. Put a number word in each sentence. Then read your sentences to someone.

Like this:

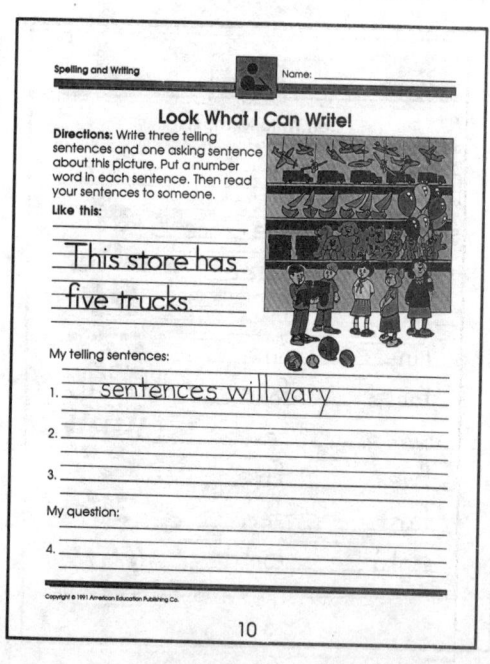

This store has five trucks

My telling sentences:

1. **sentences will vary**

2. _____

3. _____

My question:

4. _____

10

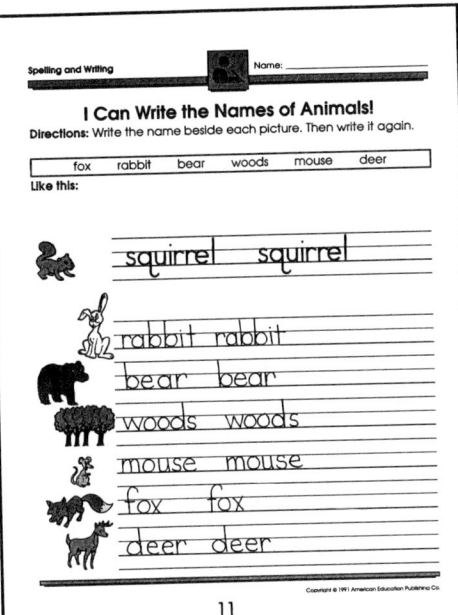

I Can Write the Names of Animals!

Directions: Write the name beside each picture. Then write it again.

fox	rabbit	bear	woods	mouse	deer

Like this:

squirrel   squirrel

rabbit   rabbit

bear   bear

woods   woods

mouse   mouse

fox   fox

deer   deer

11

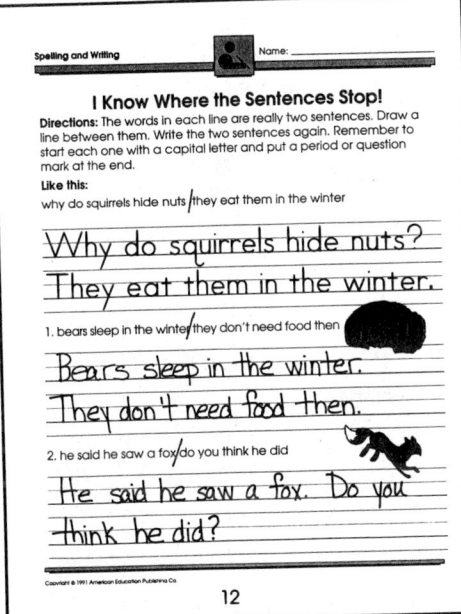

I Know Where the Sentences Stop!

Directions: The words in each line are really two sentences. Draw a line between them. Write the two sentences again. Remember to start each one with a capital letter and put a period or question mark at the end.

Like this:
why do squirrels hide nuts / they eat them in the winter

Why do squirrels hide nuts?
They eat them in the winter.

1. bears sleep in the winter / they don't need food then

Bears sleep in the winter.
They don't need food then.

2. he said he saw a fox / do you think he did

He said he saw a fox. Do you
think he did?

12

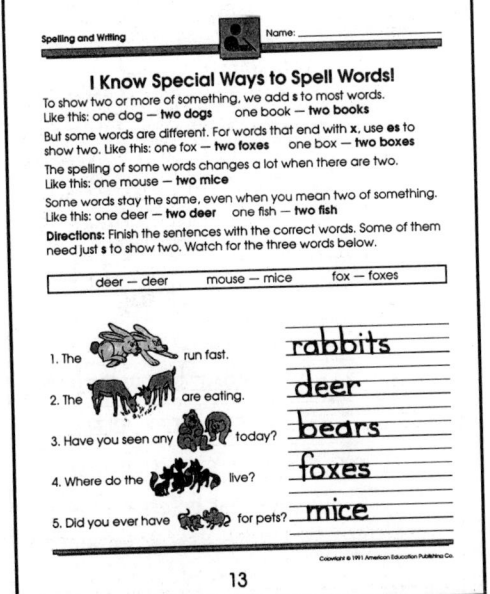

I Know Special Ways to Spell Words!

To show two or more of something, we add **s** to most words.
Like this: one dog — **two dogs**   one book — **two books**
But some words are different. For words that end with **x**, use **es** to show two. Like this: one fox — **two foxes**
The spelling of some words changes a lot when there are two.
Like this: one mouse — **two mice**
Some words stay the same, even when you mean two of something.
Like this: one deer — **two deer**   one fish — **two fish**

Directions: Finish the sentences with the correct words. Some of them need just **s** to show two. Watch for the three words below.

deer — deer	mouse — mice	fox — foxes

1. The _____ run fast. rabbits
2. The _____ are eating. deer
3. Have you seen any _____ today? bears
4. Where do the _____ live? foxes
5. Did you ever have _____ for pets? mice

13

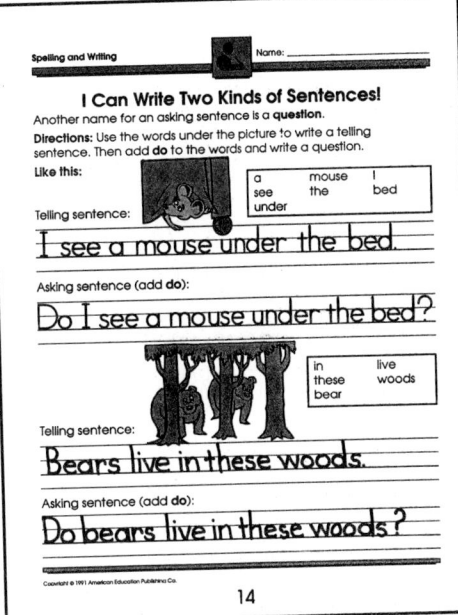

I Can Write Two Kinds of Sentences!

Another name for an asking sentence is a **question**.

Directions: Use the words under the picture to write a telling sentence. Then add **do** to the words and write a question.

Like this:

a	mouse	I
see	the	bed
under		

Telling sentence:

I see a mouse under the bed.

Asking sentence (add **do**):

Do I see a mouse under the bed?

in	live
these	woods
bear	

Telling sentence:

Bears live in these woods.

Asking sentence (add **do**):

Do bears live in these woods?

14

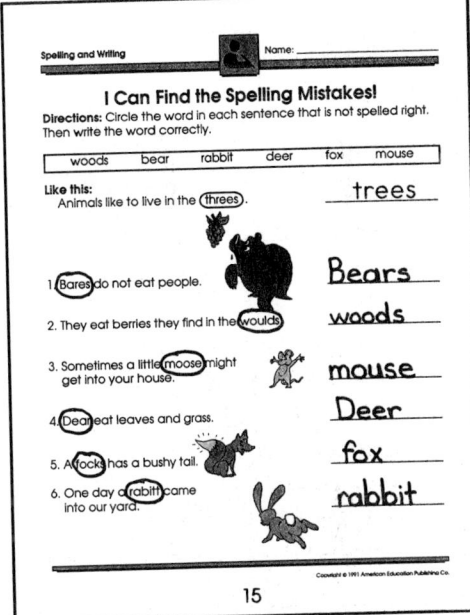

I Can Find the Spelling Mistakes!

Directions: Circle the word in each sentence that is not spelled right. Then write the word correctly.

woods	bear	rabbit	deer	fox	mouse

Like this:
Animals like to live in the (threes).   trees

1. (Bares) do not eat people.   Bears
2. They eat berries they find in the (woulds).   woods
3. Sometimes a little (moose) might get into your house.   mouse
4. (Dear) eat leaves and grass.   Deer
5. A (focks) has a bushy tail.   fox
6. One day a (rabbit) came into our yard.   rabbit

15

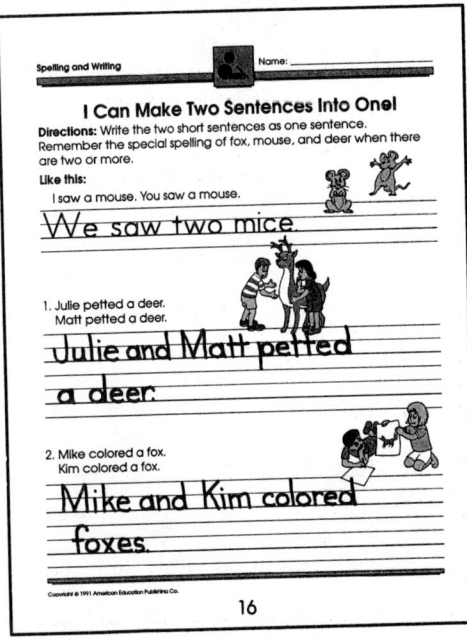

I Can Make Two Sentences Into One!

Directions: Write the two short sentences as one sentence. Remember the special spelling of fox, mouse, and deer when there are two or more.

Like this:
I saw a mouse. You saw a mouse.

We saw two mice

1. Julie petted a deer.
   Matt petted a deer.

Julie and Matt petted
a deer.

2. Mike colored a fox.
   Kim colored a fox.

Mike and Kim colored
foxes.

16

75

I Can Finish A Story!

Directions: Write the words that finish the story. Can you spell them by yourself now?

One day Kelly and I went for a walk in the **woods** near my house. Kelly was a little afraid because her big brother told her there was a **bear** in the **woods**. "Don't worry," I told Kelly. "Only **rabbits** and a **mouse** or two live here." Just then we heard a noise in the bushes. Kelly jumped, but it was just a **deer** eating leaves. "I wasn't afraid," Kelly said when she saw it was just a **deer**. "But I'm glad your dog came with us today." "I don't have a dog!" I said. "Yes, you do!" Kelly said. "He's been following us." She pointed behind me. It was a **fox**! He was just watching us, but I was a little afraid myself. "Kelly," I said quickly. "It's getting late. Let's go home!"

17

Review

Directions: Write two telling sentences and one question about the picture. Read your sentences to someone.

Like this:

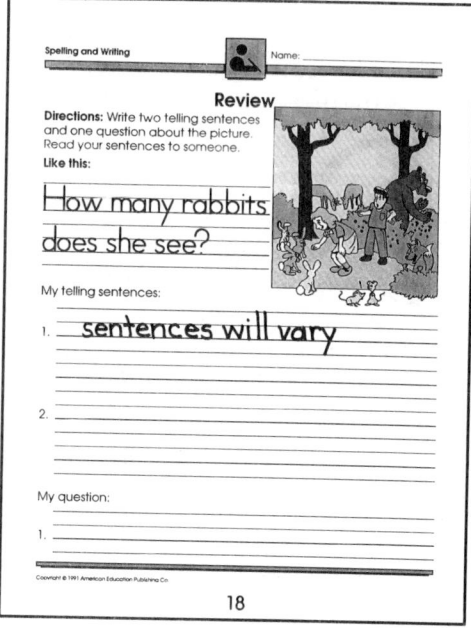

How many rabbits does she see?

My telling sentences:

1. sentences will vary

2. _____

My question:

1. _____

18

I Can Write "Family" Names!

Directions: This is Andy's **family tree**. It shows all the people in his family. Look at the pictures below that have names under them. Then find other pictures that are almost the same and write the same names under them.

grandmother   grandfather   **grandmother**   **grandfather**

aunt   uncle   my mother   my father   **aunt**   **uncle**

sister   brother   Me—Andy   **sister**   **brother**

19

76

I Can Tell About People!

Some words tell how a person looks or feels. These are also called **describing** words.

Directions: Help Andy write about the people in his family. Cross out the **describing** word that does not tell about each picture. Write a sentence that uses the other two describing words.

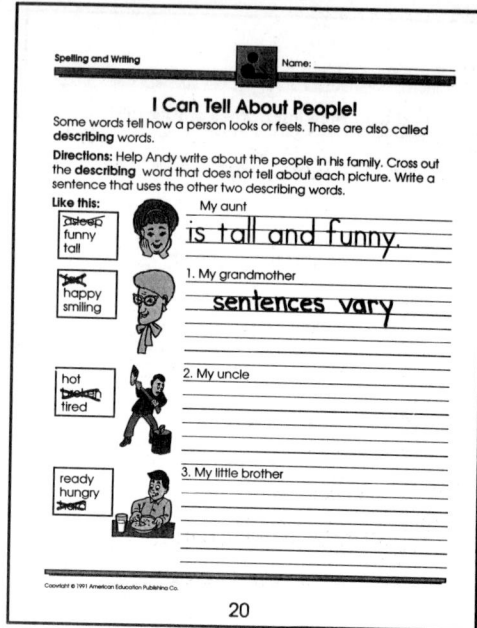

Like this:

| asleep funny tall | My aunt | is tall and funny. |

| sad happy smiling | 1. My grandmother | sentences vary |

| hot broken tired | 2. My uncle | |

| ready hungry sad | 3. My little brother | |

20

I Know Which Letters Are Vowels!

Five letters are called vowels: **a, e, i, o,** and **u.** Sometimes **y** is also a vowel. All the rest of the letters are called consonants.

Directions: 1. In the first space, the vowels for each word are written for you. Add the consonants. 2. In the second space, the consonants are written. This time you add the vowels.

grandmother   grandfather   aunt   uncle   brother   sister

Like this:

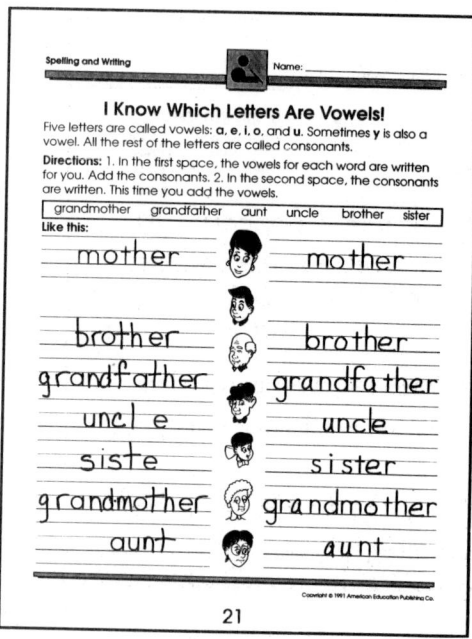

mother — mother

brother — brother
grandfather — grandfather
uncle — uncle
sister — sister
grandmother — grandmother
aunt — aunt

21

I Can Join Two Sentences!

You can join two short sentences to make one longer sentence. Three words help do this:

And —if both sentences are much the same.
Like this: I took my dog for a walk, **and** I played with my cat.

But —if the second sentence says something different from the first sentence. Sometimes the second sentence tells why you can't do the first sentence. **Like this:** I want to play outside, **but** it is raining.

Or —if each sentence names a different thing you could do.
Like this: You could eat your cookie, **or** you could give it to me.

Directions: Use the word given to join the two short sentences into one longer sentence.

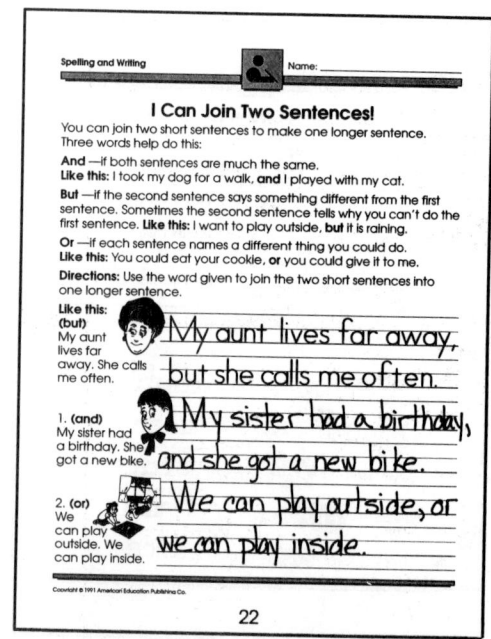

Like this:
(but)
My aunt lives far away. She calls me often.

My aunt lives far away, but she calls me often.

1. (and)
My sister had a birthday. She got a new bike.

My sister had a birthday, and she got a new bike.

2. (or)
We can play outside. We can play inside.

We can play outside, or we can play inside.

22

I Can Spell "Family" Names!

Directions: Write the correct family names in the spaces.

grandmother   grandfather   aunt   uncle   brother   sister

1. Add one or more letters to these words to spell a family word.

Like this:

fat — father

ant — aunt

is — sister

other — brother   grandmother

and her — grandfather   grandmother

2. Write the family names that start the same as these words.

Like this:

(moon) — mother

(umbrella) — uncle

(grapes) — grandmother   grandfather

23

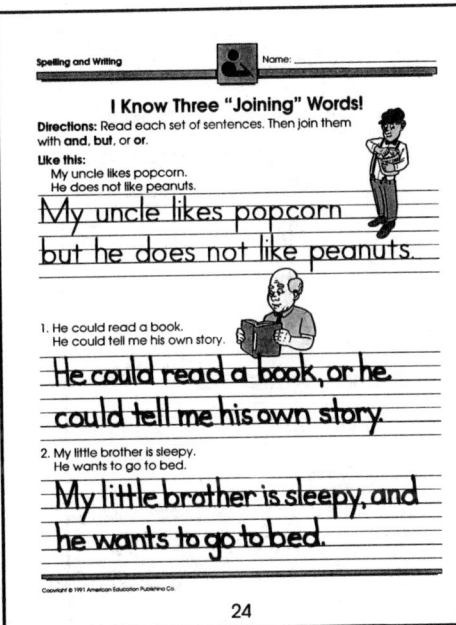

I Know Three "Joining" Words!

Directions: Read each set of sentences. Then join them with **and**, **but**, or **or**.

Like this:
My uncle likes popcorn.
He does not like peanuts.

My uncle likes popcorn but he does not like peanuts.

1. He could read a book.
He could tell me his own story.

He could read a book, or he could tell me his own story.

2. My little brother is sleepy.
He wants to go to bed.

My little brother is sleepy, and he wants to go to bed.

24

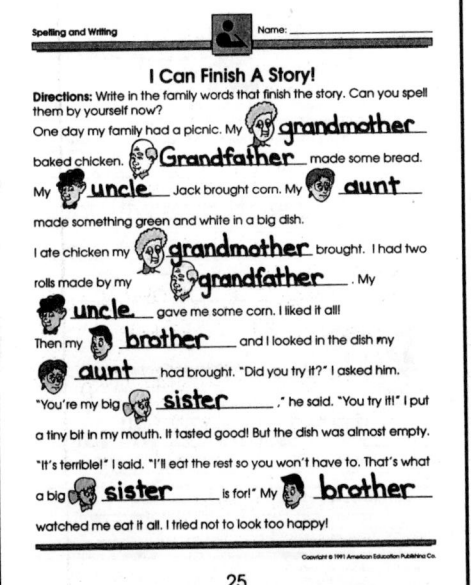

I Can Finish A Story!

Directions: Write in the family words that finish the story. Can you spell them by yourself now?

One day my family had a picnic. My grandmother baked chicken. Grandfather made some bread. My uncle Jack brought corn. My aunt made something green and white in a big dish. I ate chicken my grandmother brought. I had two rolls made by my grandfather. My uncle gave me some corn. I liked it all! Then my brother and I looked in the dish my aunt had brought. "Did you try it?" I asked him. "You're my big sister," he said. "You try it!" I put a tiny bit in my mouth. It tasted good! But the dish was almost empty.

"It's terrible!" I said. "I'll eat the rest so you won't have to. That's what a big sister is for!" My brother watched me eat it all. I tried not to look too happy!

25

Review

Directions: Draw a picture of everyone you can think of in your family. Write sentences that tell what you like about your brothers, sisters, aunts, uncles, grandmothers, and grandfathers. If you don't have any brothers or aunts or grandmothers, write a sentence telling that. (You can write more sentences on another piece of paper, if you run out of space.) Read your sentences to someone in your family.

My Family

My sentences:

sentences will vary

26

I Can Write More "Doing" Words!

Directions: Draw a line from each sentence to its picture. Then finish the sentence with the doing word that is under the picture.

Like this:
He will ___help___ the baby.

1. I can ___fix___ my book.

2. It is time to ___clean___ up.

3. That chair will ___break___.

4. They ___build___ houses.

5. I ___cut___ this out myself.

6. Is that too heavy to ___carry___?

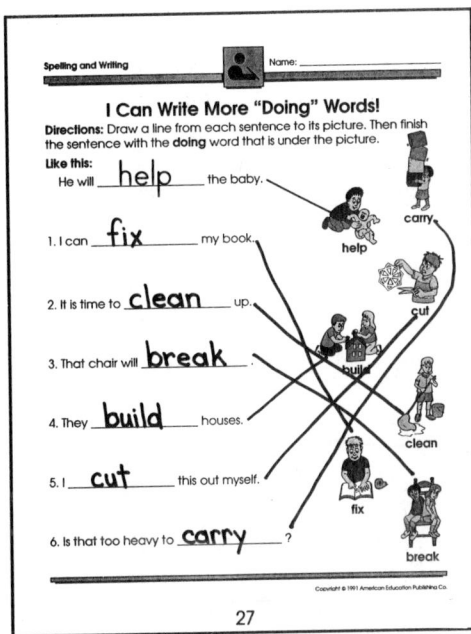

carry

help

cut

build

clean

fix

break

27

I Can Write Long Sentences!

Directions: 1. Join each pair of sentences to make one longer sentence. Use one of the joining words: **and**, **but**, or. In the second part of the sentence, use **he**, **she**, or **they** in place of a person's name.

Like this: I asked Tim to help me. Tim wanted to play.

I asked Tim to help me, but he wanted to play.

1. Kelly dropped a glass.
Kelly cut her finger.

Kelly dropped a glass, and she cut her finger.

2. Linda got a new dog.
Linda named it Baby.

Linda got a new dog, and she named it Baby.

28

Page 29

I Can Spell These "Doing" Words!

Directions: Write the correct **doing** words in the spaces.

break	build	fix	clean	cut	carry

1. Change one letter in each word to make it a **doing** word.

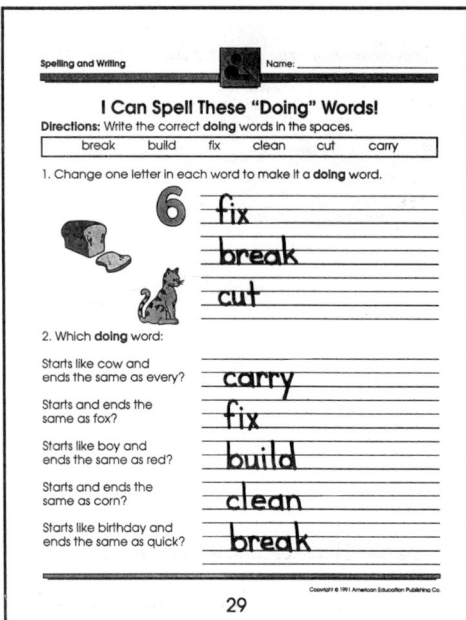

6

fix

break

cut

2. Which **doing** word:

Starts like cow and ends the same as every?   carry

Starts and ends the same as fox?   fix

Starts like boy and ends the same as red?   build

Starts and ends the same as corn?   clean

Starts like birthday and ends the same as quick?   break

Copyright © 1991 American Education Publishing Co.

29

Page 30

I Can Write What Happens!

Directions: In each story, one picture does not have a sentence. Write a sentence that tells what happened in that picture. Use one of the **doing** words.

break	build	fix	clean	cut	carry

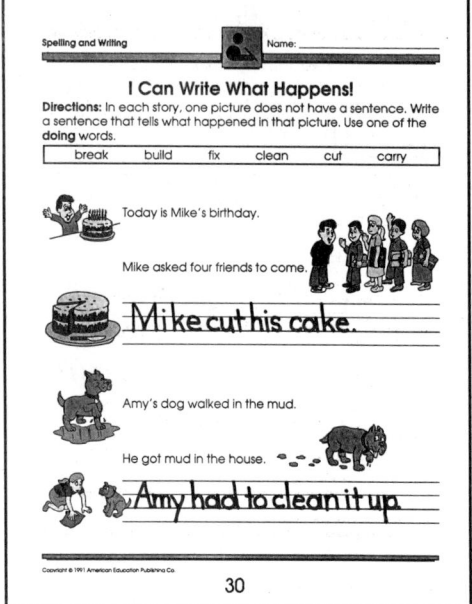

Today is Mike's birthday.

Mike asked four friends to come.

Mike cut his cake.

Amy's dog walked in the mud.

He got mud in the house.

Amy had to clean it up.

Copyright © 1991 American Education Publishing Co.

30

Page 31

I Can Change The Spelling!

Most **doing** words end with **s** when the sentence tells about one thing. The **s** is taken away when the sentence tells about more than one thing.

Like this:
One dog walks.   Two dogs walk.
One boy runs.   Three boys run.

The spelling of some **doing** words changes when the sentence tells about only one thing.

Like this:
One girl carries her lunch.   Two girls carry their lunches.
The boy fixes his car.   Two boys fix their cars.
(The spelling for fix and fixes is just like fox and foxes.)

Directions: Write the missing **doing** words in the sentences.

Like this:
Pam works hard. She and Peter __work__ all day.

1. The father bird builds a nest. 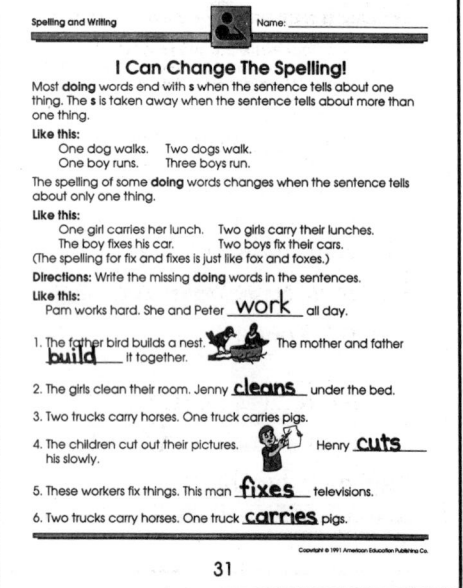 The mother and father __build__ it together.

2. The girls clean their room. Jenny __cleans__ under the bed.

3. Two trucks carry horses. One truck carries pigs.

4. The children cut out their pictures. Henry __cuts__ his slowly.

5. These workers fix things. This man __fixes__ televisions.

6. Two trucks carry horses. One truck __carries__ pigs.

Copyright © 1991 American Education Publishing Co.

31

Page 32

I Can Tell A Story!

Directions: Write a sentence that tells what happens in each picture. Use the **doing** word printed under the picture. Remember the spelling changes in the lesson on page 29. Read your story to someone.

Like this:

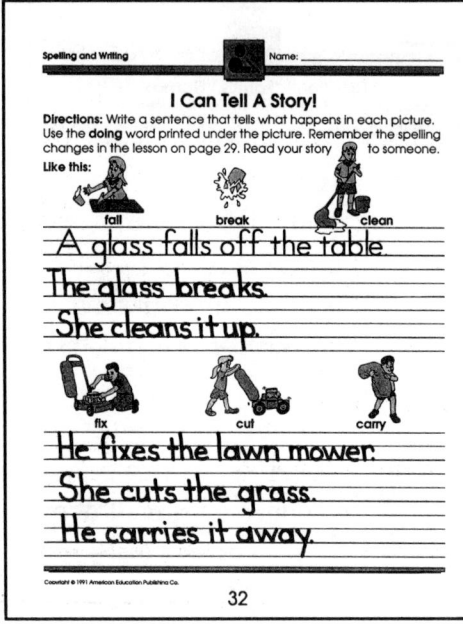

fall   break   clean

A glass falls off the table.

The glass breaks.

She cleans it up.

fix   cut   carry

He fixes the lawn mower.

She cuts the grass.

He carries it away.

Copyright © 1991 American Education Publishing Co.

32

Page 33

I Can Find the Spelling Mistakes!

Directions: Circle the two spelling mistakes in each sentence. Then write the sentence correctly. Watch for mistakes in **doing** words, family names, animals, and numbers. Can you spell the words by yourself now?

Like this:
I need to (klean) the cage my (mouses) live in.

I need to clean the cage my mice live in.

2. The chair will (brake) if (tree) of us sit on it.

The chair will break if three of us sit on it.

3. A mother (bare) (carry) her baby in her mouth.

A mother bear carries her baby in her mouth.

Copyright © 1991 American Education Publishing Co.

33

Page 34

Review

Directions: Write sentences that answer the questions under each picture. Be sure to use the **doing** words.

What will happen here? What will the boy do next?

sentences will vary

How is the girl helping? What will happen next?

sentences will vary

Copyright © 1991 American Education Publishing Co.

34

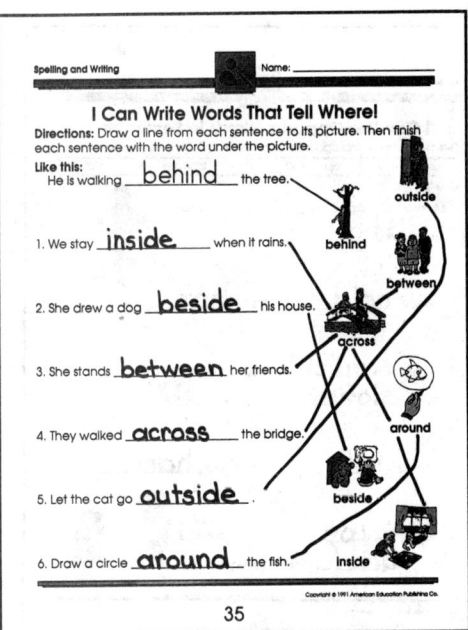

I Can Write Words That Tell Where!

Directions: Draw a line from each sentence to its picture. Then finish each sentence with the word under the picture.

Like this:
He is walking __behind__ the tree.

1. We stay __inside__ when it rains.

2. She drew a dog __beside__ his house.

3. She stands __between__ her friends.

4. They walked __across__ the bridge.

5. Let the cat go __outside__ .

6. Draw a circle __around__ the fish.

outside
behind
between
across
around
beside
inside

Copyright © 1991 American Education Publishing Co.

35

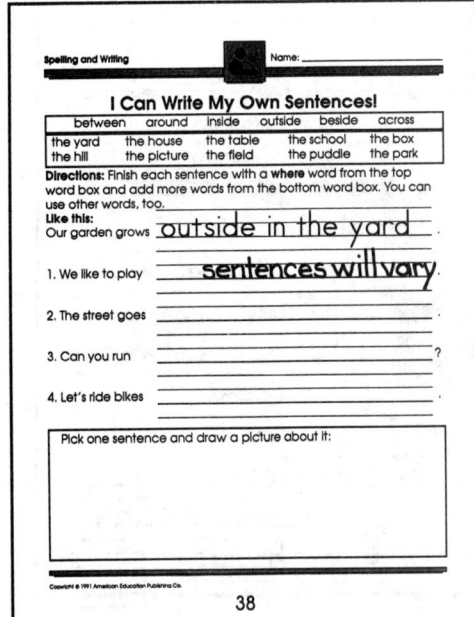

I Can Write My Own Sentences!

between	around	inside	outside	beside	across
the yard	the house	the table	the school	the box
the hill	the picture	the field	the puddle	the park

Directions: Finish each sentence with a **where** word from the top word box and add more words from the bottom word box. You can use other words, too.

Like this:
Our garden grows __outside in the yard__

1. We like to play __sentences will vary__ .

2. The street goes _____

3. Can you run _____ ?

4. Let's ride bikes _____

Pick one sentence and draw a picture about it:

Copyright © 1991 American Education Publishing Co.

38

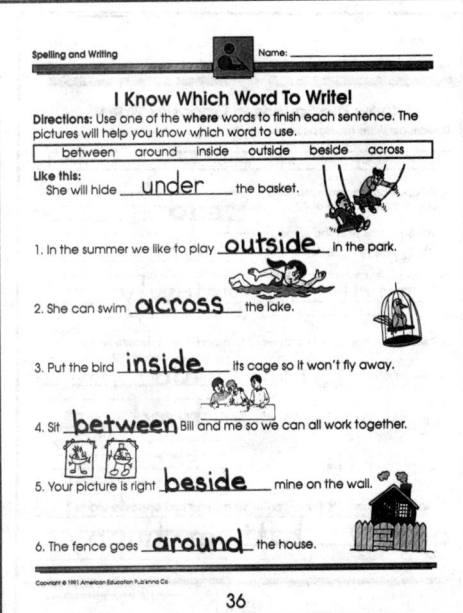

I Know Which Word To Write!

Directions: Use one of the **where** words to finish each sentence. The pictures will help you know which word to use.

between	around	inside	outside	beside	across

Like this:
She will hide __under__ the basket.

1. In the summer we like to play __outside__ in the park.

2. She can swim __across__ the lake.

3. Put the bird __inside__ its cage so it won't fly away.

4. Sit __between__ Bill and me so we can all work together.

5. Your picture is right __beside__ mine on the wall.

6. The fence goes __around__ the house.

Copyright © 1991 American Education Publishing Co.

36

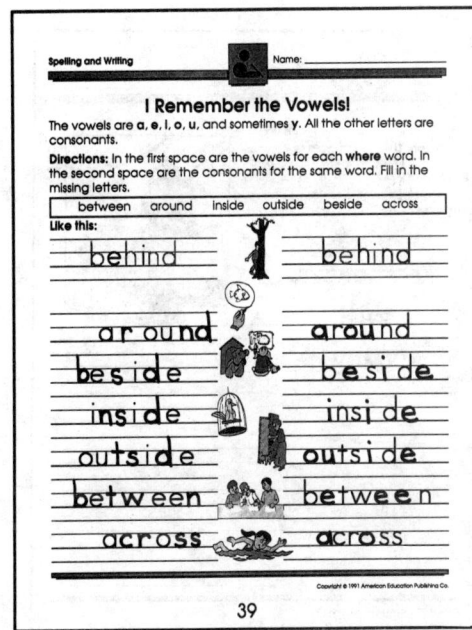

I Remember the Vowels!

The vowels are **a, e, i, o, u,** and sometimes **y.** All the other letters are consonants.

Directions: In the first space are the vowels for each **where** word. In the second space are the consonants for the same word. Fill in the missing letters.

between	around	inside	outside	beside	across

Like this:

behind   behind

around   around

beside   beside

inside   inside

outside   outside

between   between

across   across

Copyright © 1991 American Education Publishing Co.

39

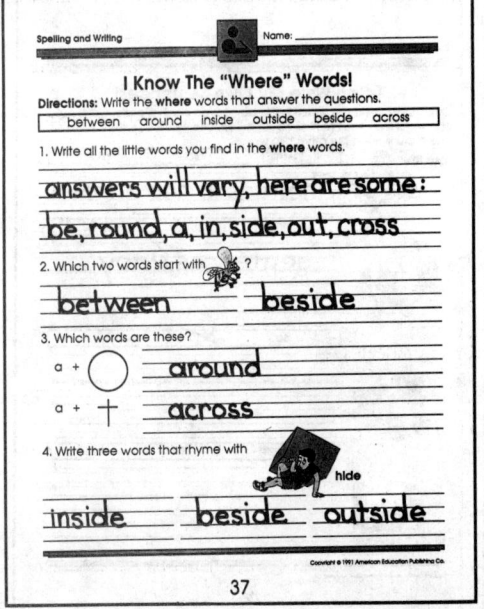

I Know The "Where" Words!

Directions: Write the **where** words that answer the questions.

between	around	inside	outside	beside	across

1. Write all the little words you find in the **where** words.

__answers will vary, here are some :__
__be, round, a, in, side, out, cross__

2. Which two words start with __B__ ?

__between__   __beside__

3. Which words are these?

a + ◯   __around__

a + ✝   __across__

4. Write three words that rhyme with _hide_

__inside__   __beside__   __outside__

Copyright © 1991 American Education Publishing Co.

37

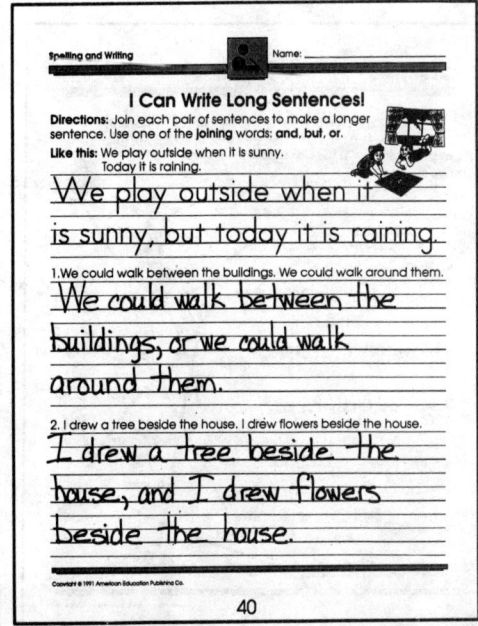

I Can Write Long Sentences!

Directions: Join each pair of sentences to make a longer sentence. Use one of the **joining** words: and, but, or.

Like this: We play outside when it is sunny.
Today it is raining.

__We play outside when it is sunny, but today it is raining.__

1. We could walk between the buildings. We could walk around them.

__We could walk between the buildings, or we could walk around them.__

2. I drew a tree beside the house. I drew flowers beside the house.

__I drew a tree beside the house, and I drew flowers beside the house.__

Copyright © 1991 American Education Publishing Co.

40

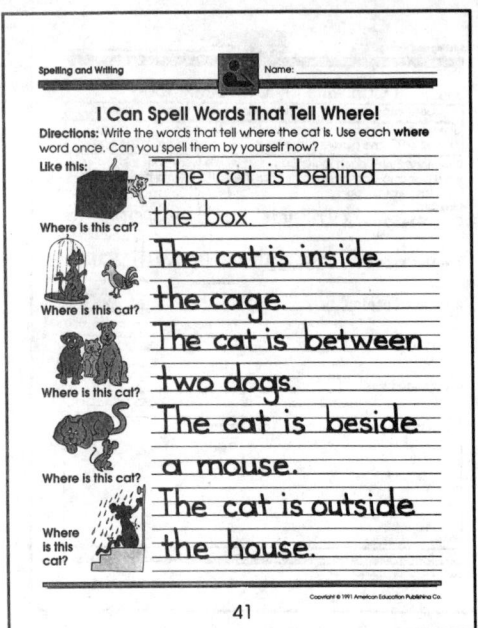

I Can Spell Words That Tell Where!

Directions: Write the words that tell where the cat is. Use each **where** word once. Can you spell them by yourself now?

Like this:

The cat is behind the box.

Where is this cat?

The cat is inside the cage.

Where is this cat?

The cat is between two dogs.

Where is this cat?

The cat is beside a mouse.

Where is this cat?

The cat is outside the house.

Where is this cat?

41

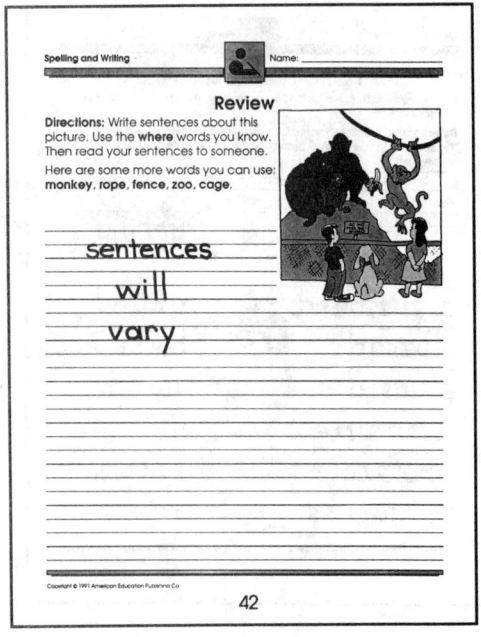

Review

Directions: Write sentences about this picture. Use the **where** words you know. Then read your sentences to someone.

Here are some more words you can use: **monkey, rope, fence, zoo, cage.**

sentences will vary

42

I Can Write More "Opposite" Words!

Directions: Draw a line from each sentence to its picture. Then finish each sentence with the word under the picture.

Like this:
She bought a **new** bat.

1. I like my **soft** pillow.

2. Birthdays make me **happy**.

3. Put that book on **top**.

4. Jenny runs **quickly**.

5. A rock makes a **hard** seat.

6. I feel **sad** when it rains.

7. He eats **slowly**.

hard
new
top
sad
slowly
quickly
happy
soft

43

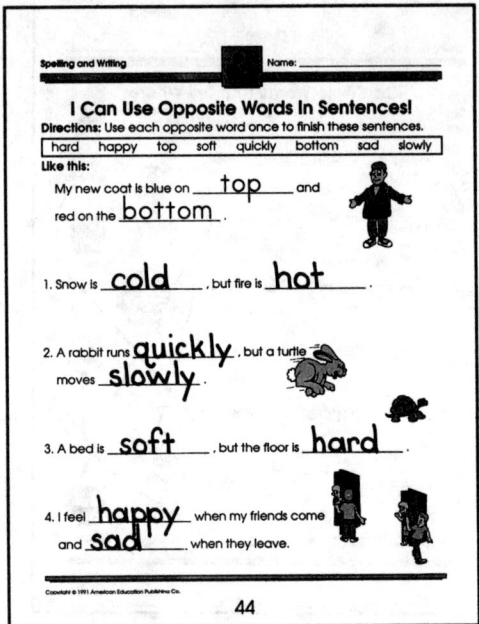

I Can Use Opposite Words In Sentences!

Directions: Use each opposite word once to finish these sentences.

| hard | happy | top | soft | quickly | bottom | sad | slowly |

Like this:
My new coat is blue on **top** and red on the **bottom**.

1. Snow is **cold**, but fire is **hot**.

2. A rabbit runs **quickly**, but a turtle moves **slowly**.

3. A bed is **soft**, but the floor is **hard**.

4. I feel **happy** when my friends come and **sad** when they leave.

44

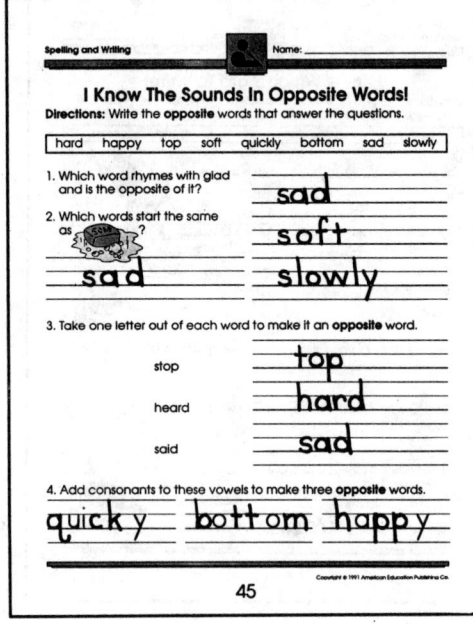

I Know The Sounds In Opposite Words!

Directions: Write the **opposite** words that answer the questions.

| hard | happy | top | soft | quickly | bottom | sad | slowly |

1. Which word rhymes with glad and is the opposite of it?
sad

2. Which words start the same as ____ ?
soft
sad   **slowly**

3. Take one letter out of each word to make it an **opposite** word.

stop **top**

heard **hard**

said **sad**

4. Add consonants to these vowels to make three **opposite** words.

quicky **bottom** **happy**

45

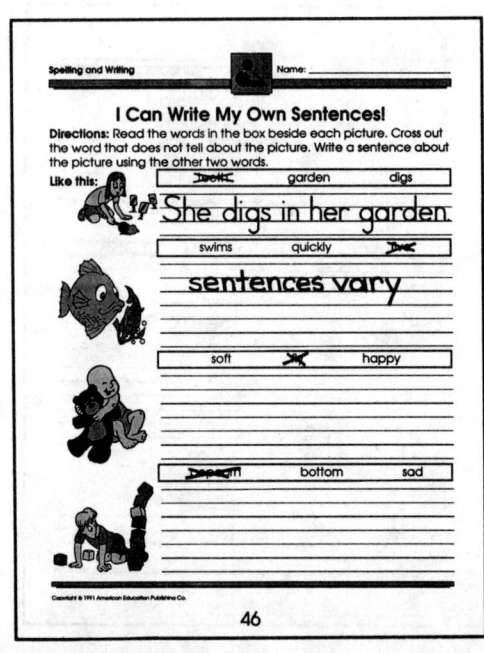

I Can Write My Own Sentences!

Directions: Read the words in the box beside each picture. Cross out the word that does not tell about the picture. Write a sentence about the picture using the other two words.

Like this:

| ~~soft~~ | garden | digs |

She digs in her garden.

| swims | quickly | ~~fix~~ |

sentences vary

| soft | ~~fly~~ | happy |

| ~~clean~~ | bottom | sad |

46

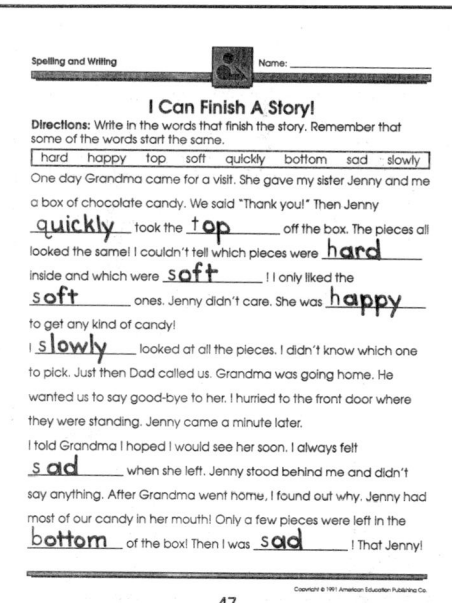

I Can Finish A Story!

Directions: Write in the words that finish the story. Remember that some of the words start the same.

| hard | happy | top | soft | quickly | bottom | sad | slowly |

One day Grandma came for a visit. She gave my sister Jenny and me a box of chocolate candy. We said "Thank you!" Then Jenny **quickly** took the **top** off the box. The pieces all looked the same! I couldn't tell which pieces were **hard** inside and which were **soft** ! I only liked the **soft** ones. Jenny didn't care. She was **happy** to get any kind of candy!

I **slowly** looked at all the pieces. I didn't know which one to pick. Just then Dad called us. Grandma was going home. He wanted us to say good-bye to her. I hurried to the front door where they were standing. Jenny came a minute later.

I told Grandma I hoped I would see her soon. I always felt **sad** when she left. Jenny stood behind me and didn't say anything. After Grandma went home, I found out why. Jenny had most of our candy in her mouth! Only a few pieces were left in the **bottom** of the box! Then I was **sad** ! That Jenny!

47

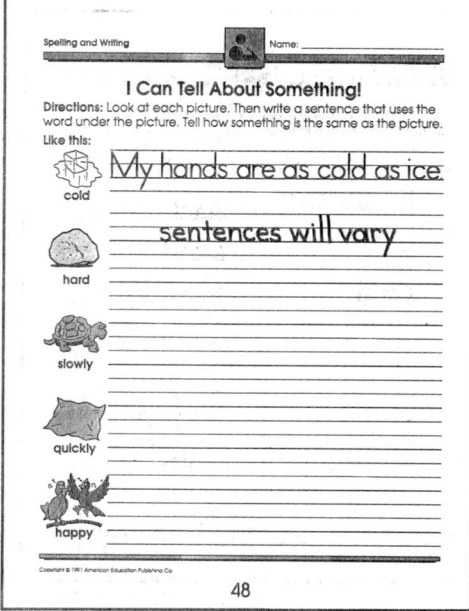

I Can Tell About Something!

Directions: Look at each picture. Then write a sentence that uses the word under the picture. Tell how something is the same as the picture.

Like this:

cold — My hands are as cold as ice.

hard — sentences will vary

slowly —

quickly —

happy —

48

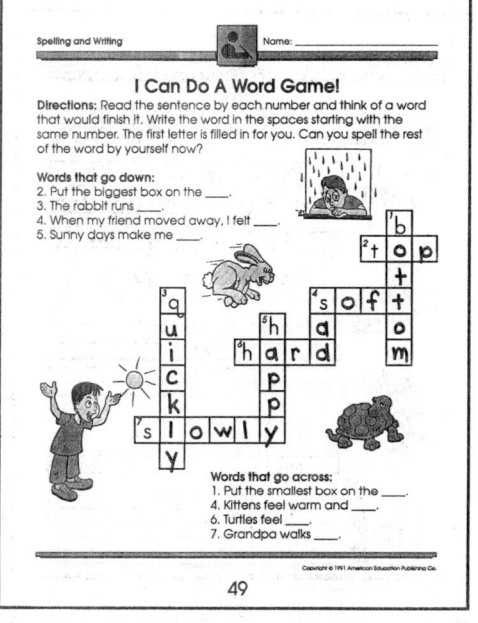

I Can Do A Word Game!

Directions: Read the sentence by each number and think of a word that would finish it. Write the word in the spaces starting with the same number. The first letter is filled in for you. Can you spell the rest of the word by yourself now?

Words that go down:
2. Put the biggest box on the ___.
3. The rabbit runs ___.
4. When my friend moved away, I felt ___.
5. Sunny days make me ___.

Words that go across:
1. Put the smallest box on the ___.
4. Kittens feel warm and ___.
6. Turtles feel ___.
7. Grandpa walks ___.

49

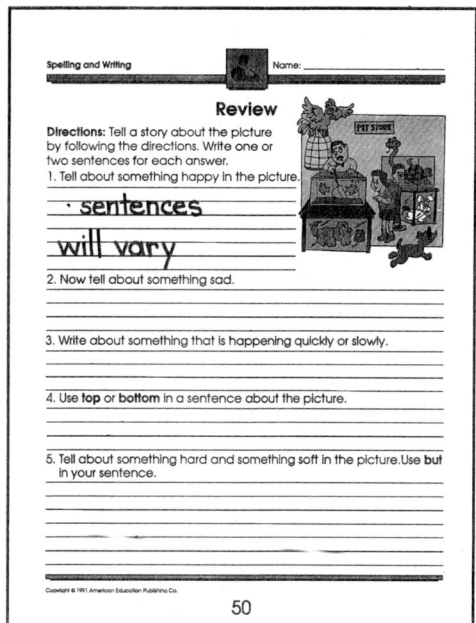

Review

Directions: Tell a story about the picture by following the directions. Write one or two sentences for each answer.
1. Tell about something happy in the picture.

sentences will vary

2. Now tell about something sad.

3. Write about something that is happening quickly or slowly.

4. Use **top** or **bottom** in a sentence about the picture.

5. Tell about something hard and something soft in the picture. Use **but** in your sentence.

50

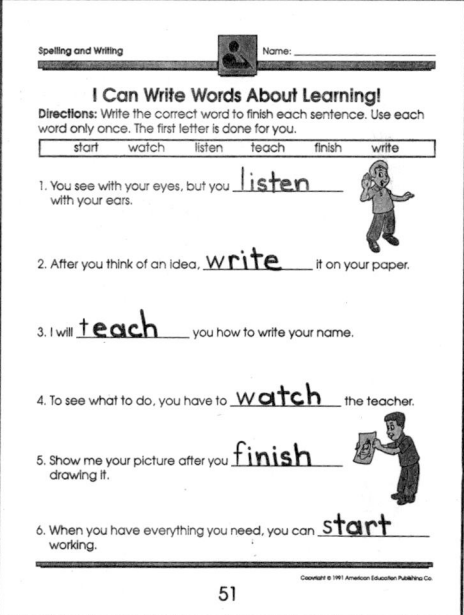

I Can Write Words About Learning!

Directions: Write the correct word to finish each sentence. Use each word only once. The first letter is done for you.

| start | watch | listen | teach | finish | write |

1. You see with your eyes, but you **listen** with your ears.

2. After you think of an idea, **write** it on your paper.

3. I will **teach** you how to write your name.

4. To see what to do, you have to **watch** the teacher.

5. Show me your picture after you **finish** drawing it.

6. When you have everything you need, you can **start** working.

51

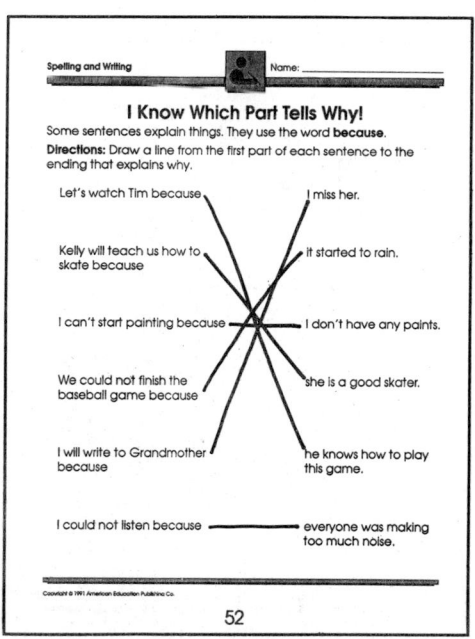

I Know Which Part Tells Why!

Some sentences explain things. They use the word **because**.
Directions: Draw a line from the first part of each sentence to the ending that explains why.

Let's watch Tim because — I miss her.

Kelly will teach us how to skate because — it started to rain.

I can't start painting because — I don't have any paints.

We could not finish the baseball game because — she is a good skater.

I will write to Grandmother because — he knows how to play this game.

I could not listen because — everyone was making too much noise.

52

Spelling I Can Spell Words About Learning!

Directions: Write the words that answer the questions.

start	watch	listen	teach	finish	write

Which words are not spelled correctly? Circle them and then write them correctly.

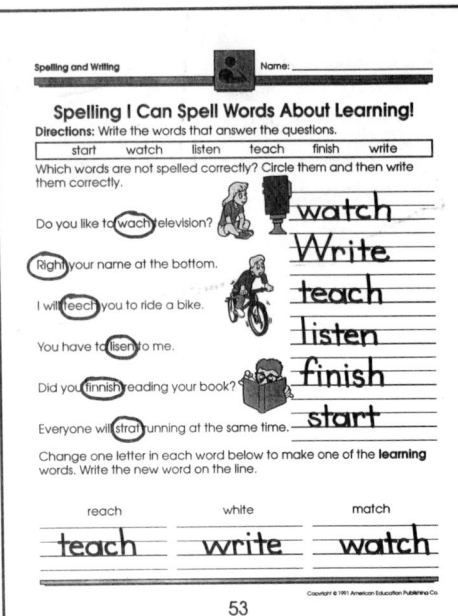

Do you like to (watch) television? — **watch**

(Right) your name at the bottom. — **Write**

I will (teach) you to ride a bike. — **teach**

You have to (lisen) to me. — **listen**

Did you (finnish) reading your book? — **finish**

Everyone will (strat) running at the same time. — **start**

Change one letter in each word below to make one of the **learning** words. Write the new word on the line.

reach   white   match

teach   **write**   **watch**

53

I Can Tell Why!

Directions: Write your own ending to the sentences below. Tell why something happened.

Like this:
I will read this book because

I like stories about baseball.

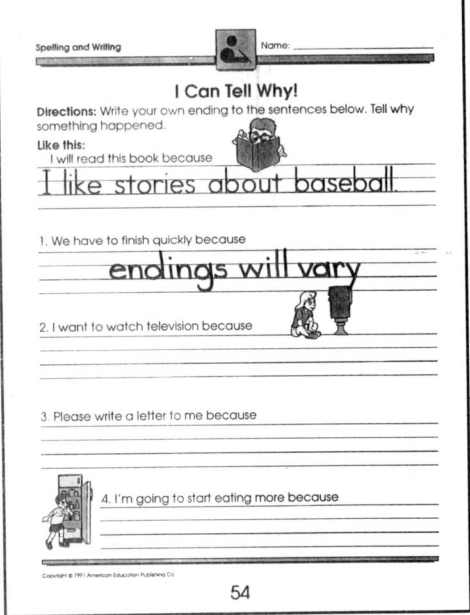

1. We have to finish quickly because

endings will vary

2. I want to watch television because

_____

3. Please write a letter to me because

_____

4. I'm going to start eating more because

_____

54

I Know Different Ways To End Words!

Remember that **doing** words end with **s** when the sentence tells about only one thing.

Like this: One girl reads.   Two girls read.

But when a **doing** word ends with **ch** or **sh**, add **es**.

Like this: She watches the baby.   We watch the baby, too.
Peter finishes his work.   Jane and Sue finish their work.

Directions: Write the word that finishes each sentence.

Like this:
Carrie reads the book. She and Chris **read** it together.

start	watch	listen	teach	finish	write

1. Todd listens to the teacher. We all **listen** to her.

2. Joy finishes the race first. We **finish** after her.

3. They write letters to our class. Tony **writes** back to them.

4. We watch the puppet show. She **watches** with us.

5. He starts at the top of the page. We **start** in the middle.

55

I Can Write My Own Sentences!

Directions: Write your own sentences. Use a word from each box and add more words of your own to finish your sentences. Add **s** or **es** to the end of the **doing** words if you need to. Use **because** in one of your sentences. Draw a picture to show what is happening in one sentence.

teach	write	listen	watch	start	finish
We	She	They	He	Kenny	Susan
Tammy	Henry	(other names you know)			

Like this:

1. Robert watches the race

2. sentences will vary

3. _____

4. _____

Draw your picture here:

56

I Can Finish A Story!

Directions: Write in the **learning** words that finish this story. The first letter of each one is written for you. Can you spell the rest by yourself?

"How can I **teach** you anything if you don't **listen** ?" James asked his little sister Wendy. He was trying to show her how to **write** her name. Wendy smiled up at James. "I'll **listen** now," she said. "Okay. Let's **start** again. **Watch** what I do," he said.

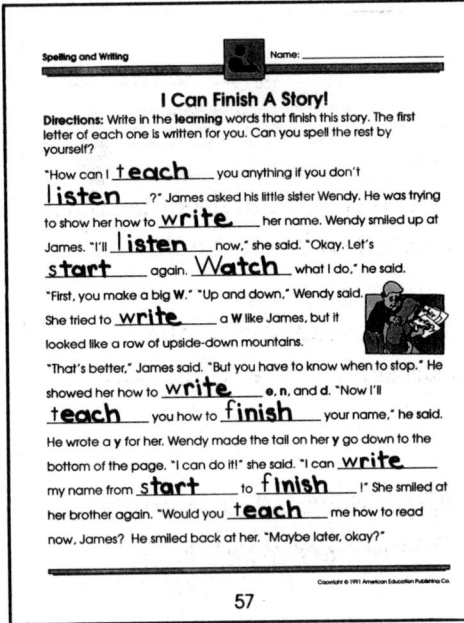

"First, you make a big **W**." "Up and down," Wendy said. She tried to **write** a W like James, but it looked like a row of upside-down mountains.

"That's better," James said. "But you have to know when to stop." He showed her how to **write** e, n, and d. "Now I'll **teach** you how to **finish** your name," he said. He wrote a **y** for her. Wendy made the tail on her **y** go down to the bottom of the page. "I can do it!" she said. "I can **write** my name from **start** to **finish** !" She smiled at her brother again. "Would you **teach** me how to read now, James? He smiled back at her. "Maybe later, okay?"

57

Review

Directions: Answer the questions below to tell your own story about this picture. Use the **learning** words you know.

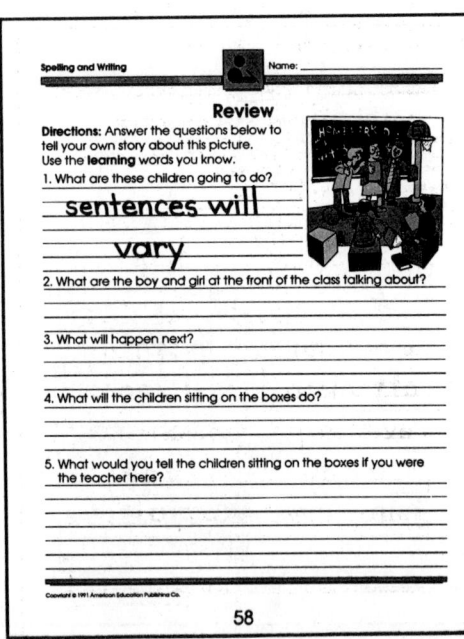

1. What are these children going to do?

sentences will vary

2. What are the boy and girl at the front of the class talking about?

_____

3. What will happen next?

_____

4. What will the children sitting on the boxes do?

_____

5. What would you tell the children sitting on the boxes if you were the teacher here?

_____

58

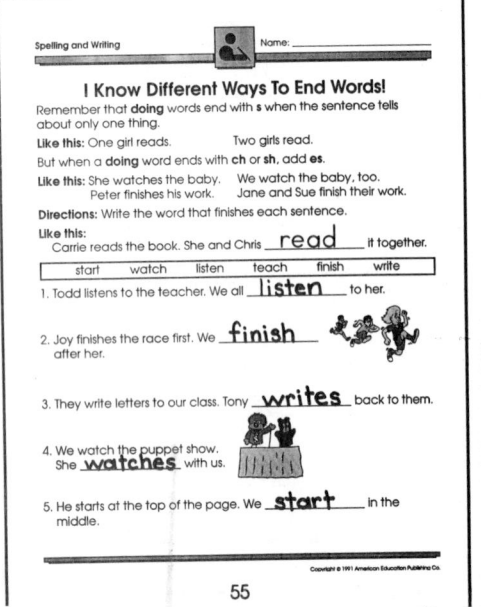

I Can Write "Time" Words!

The time between breakfast and lunch is **morning**.
The time between lunch and dinner is **afternoon**.
The time between dinner and bedtime is **evening**.

Directions: Write the correct word to finish each sentence. Use each word only once.

morning	afternoon	evening	today	tomorrow

1. What did you eat for breakfast this **morning** ?

2. We come home from school in the **afternoon** .

3. I help wash the dinner dishes in the **evening** .

4. I feel a little tired **today** .

5. If I rest tonight, I will feel better **tomorrow** .

59

I Can Write My Own Sentences!

Directions: Write a sentence for these **time** words. Tell something you do at that time.

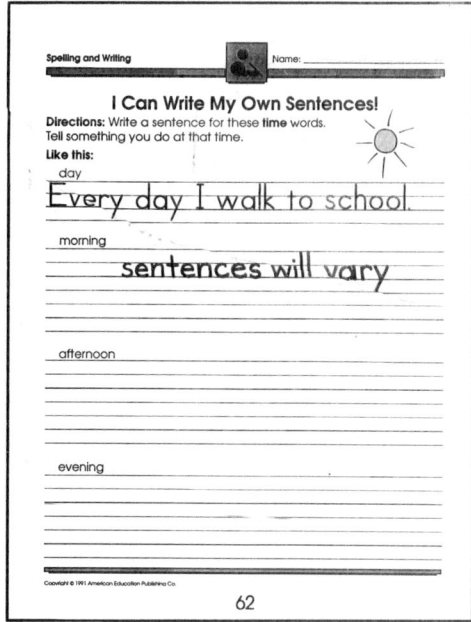

Like this:

day

Every day I walk to school.

morning

sentences will vary

afternoon

evening

62

I Can Write Long Sentences!

Directions: Make each pair of short sentences into one long sentence. Use these **joining** words: and, but, or, because.

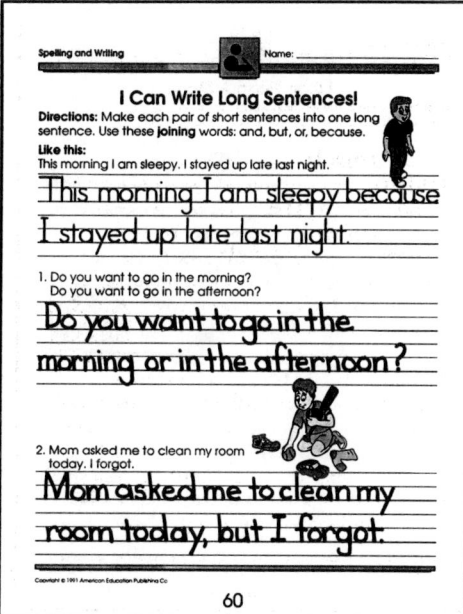

Like this:
This morning I am sleepy. I stayed up late last night.

This morning I am sleepy because I stayed up late last night.

1. Do you want to go in the morning?
   Do you want to go in the afternoon?

Do you want to go in the morning or in the afternoon?

2. Mom asked me to clean my room today. I forgot.

Mom asked me to clean my room today, but I forgot.

60

I Can Do A Word Game!

Directions: The words by each number tell about one of the **time** words. Write the right **time** word by the same number in the game. Can you spell the words by yourself now?

The word that goes down:
1. The time between lunch and dinner

The words that go across:
2. This day
3. The next day
4. The time between breakfast and lunch
5. The time between lunch and bedtime

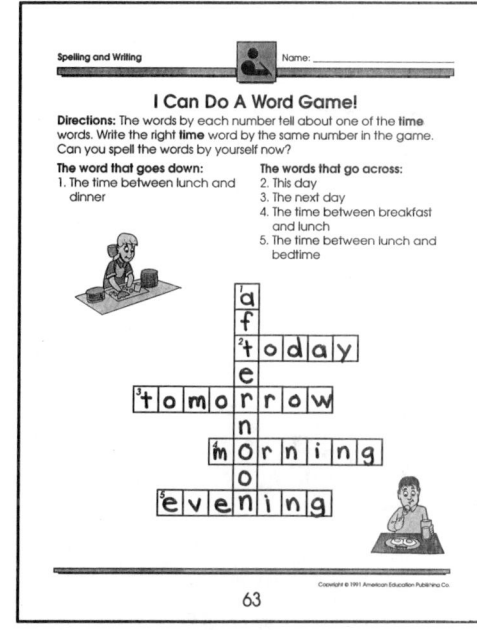

Crossword answers:
- a f
- 2. t o d a y
- e
- 3. t o m o r r o w
- n
- 4. m o r n i n g
- o
- 5. e v e n i n g

63

I Know Vowels and Consonants!

Directions: The vowels for each **time** word are written on the first space. The consonants for the same word are on the second space. Write in the missing letters for all the words.

Like this:

morning	afternoon	evening	today	tomorrow

night   night

morning	morning
afternoon	afte rnoon
evening	evening
today	today
tomorrow	tomorrow

61

Review

Directions: Write the story below again and fix all the mistakes. Watch for: words that aren't spelled right; missing periods and question marks; question marks at the end of telling sentences; sentences with the wrong **joining** words. If needed, use your own paper, too.

One **mourning** my **granmother** said I could have a pet mouse. She would **teech** me how to take care of it. First, she helped me **bild** a **cage. I** said I would keep it very **klean?**

That evenening we got my mouse at the pet store, the next **afernoon** my mouse had babies! Now I had **nyne mouses**! I really liked to **wach** them? I wanted to pick the babies up, **and** they were too **litlle.**

When they get bigger, I have to give **too mouses** to my **sisster.** Maybe her **mouses** will have babies, but we will have more **mouses**!

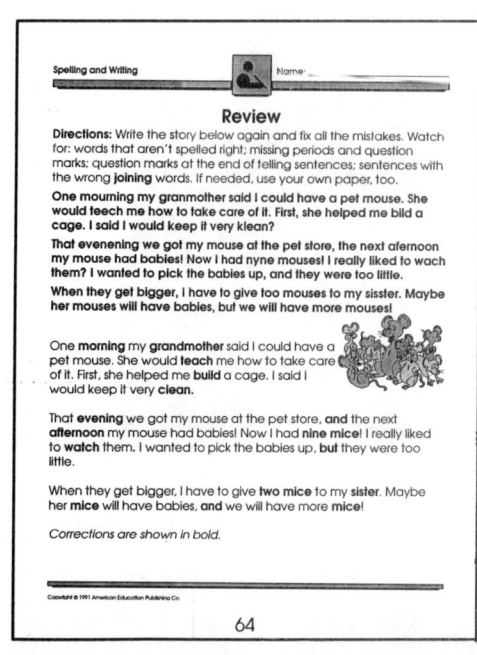

One **morning** my **grandmother** said I could have a pet mouse. She would **teach** me how to take care of it. First, she helped me **build** a cage. I said I would keep it very **clean.**

That **evening** we got my mouse at the pet store, **and** the next **afternoon** my mouse had babies! Now I had **nine mice!** I really liked to **watch** them. I wanted to pick the babies up, **but** they were too little.

When they get bigger, I have to give **two mice** to my **sister.** Maybe her **mice** will have babies, **and** we will have more **mice!**

Corrections are shown in bold.

64

OVERVIEW

ENRICHMENT READING is designed to provide children with practice in reading and to increase students' reading abilities. The program consists of six editions, one each for grades 1 through 6. The major areas of reading instruction--word skills, vocabulary, study skills, comprehension, and literary forms--are covered as appropriate at each level.

ENRICHMENT READING provides a wide range of activities that target a variety of skills in each instructional area. The program is unique because it helps children expand their skills in playful ways with games, puzzles, riddles, contests, and stories. The high-interest activities are informative and fun to do.

Home involvement is important to any child's success in school. *ENRICHMENT READING* is the ideal vehicle for fostering home involvement. Every lesson provides specific opportunities for children to work with a parent, a family member, an adult, or a friend.

AUTHORS

Peggy Kaye, the author of *ENRICHMENT READING*, is also an author of *ENRICHMENT MATH* and the author of two parent/teacher resource books, *Games for Reading* and *Games for Math*. Currently, Ms. Kaye divides her time between writing books and tutoring students in reading and math. She has also taught for ten years in New York City public and private schools.

WRITERS

Timothy J. Baehr is a writer and editor of instructional materials on the elementary, secondary, and college levels. Mr. Baehr has also authored an award-winning column on bicycling and a resource book for writers of educational materials.

Cynthia Benjamin is a writer of reading instructional materials, television scripts, and original stories. Ms. Benjamin has also tutored students in reading at the New York University Reading Institute.

Russell Ginns is a writer and editor of materials for a children's science and nature magazine. Mr. Ginn's speciality is interactive materials, including games, puzzles, and quizzes.

WHY ENRICHMENT READING?

Enrichment and parental involvement are both crucial to children's success in school, and educators recognize the important role work done at home plays in the educational process. Enrichment activities give children opportunities to practice, apply, and expand their reading skills, while encouraging them to think while they read. *ENRICHMENT READING* offers exactly this kind of opportunity. Each lesson focuses on an important reading skill and involves children in active learning. Each lesson will entertain and delight children.

When childen enjoy their lessons and are involved in the activities, they are naturally alert and receptive to learning. They understand more. They remember more. All children enjoy playing games, having contests, and solving puzzles. They like reading interesting stories, amusing stories, jokes, and riddles. Activities such as these get children involved in reading. This is why these kinds of activities form the core of *ENRICHMENT READING*.

Each lesson consists of two parts. Children complete the first part by themselves. The second part is completed together with a family member, an adult, or a friend. *ENRICHMENT READING* activities do not require people at home to teach reading. Instead, the activities involve everyone in enjoyable reading games and interesting language experiences.

Page 65   Answers and stories will vary, but should include details from the picture.

Page 66   Ideas will vary, but should tell what might happen next in the story.

Page 67   Answers will vary.

Page 68   *First story:* true *Second story:* true *Third story:* not true

Page 69   Stories will vary.

Page 70   Answers will vary.

Page 71   *Top row:* Goo, Roo, Roo *Bottom row:* Goo, Goo, Roo

Page 72   Results will vary.